THE DESSERT KITCHEN

Fruity, Chocolatey & Scrummy

150

GREAT RECIPES

★ CONTENTS

★

★

INTRODUCTION

Saving room for dessert? If you think one of the best things about going out for dinner is the dessert menu, then this is the book for you. Because why wait for a night out, when it's simple and fun to recreate your favourite desserts at home. With over 150 easy and delicious recipes to choose from, there is something here for everyone. And you don't have to be an accomplished cook or baker to do it either. Mouthwatering, delicious and decadent desserts are just a dollop of cream and a whisk of butter and sugar away.

This book kicks off with the Classic section, equipping you with go-to recipes for desserts that you really feel you ought to know how to make. That's apple pie, chocolate fondant pudding, cheesecake, rice pudding, creme brulee, poached pears or a fruit crumble. If you are looking for a simple staple that's reliable and tastes great, you'll find it in this section of the book.

For some people, dessert is just not dessert without chocolate. If that describes you, or someone in your family, help is at hand in the Chocolate Lovers section of this book. Here you'll find a recipe to satisfy even the hardest chocolate craving. We've got all the obvious ones ticked off: a sumptuous chocolate loaf cake, creamy chocolate truffles, fluffy chocolate mousses and a winning chocolate cherry pavlova. And, if you fancy something challenging, we have recipes to help raise the bar on your dessert-making skills. How about homemade chocolate doughnuts, chocolate rum baba or chocolate and raspberry ice cream cookies? Seems salted caramel is chocolate's best friend these days, so why not try the chocolate brownies with salted caramel sauce or salted caramel and chocolate meringues?

If fruit's more your thing, then fast forward to the Fruity Favourites section of this book where you'll discover many recipes to sample and savour. Apples and red fruit lend the basis to many classic desserts, such as pies, flans, tarts and crumbles, and you'll find some easy and interesting variations on this theme. Learn how to stew rhubarb and make a simple crumble and you'll have dessert done and dusted in 20 minutes. Or spend a little longer to create a buttery and beautiful cherry clafoutis, or homemade apple strudel that your loved ones are sure to thank you for. Tangy, zesty citrus is the main act in a range of summery desserts from panna cotta with orange jelly to lemon posset and lemon cream cake.

In the next section, we celebrate the current appetite for all things frozen. You'll find kid-friendly and easy-peasy recipes in here for ice pops and ice cream. With a little more time and effort, you can learn how to make frozen versions of some classic desserts such as mousse cake and cheesecake. Also in this section you'll find a recipe for the classic frozen semifreddo, a rich indulgent dessert that's perfect for a dinner party.

For everyday desserts, hop straight to the Easy section for awesome ideas for whipping up fast and simple desserts that will be a hit with adults and kids alike. Banana splits, knickerbocker glories, marshmallow skewers and Dutch pancakes are winning ideas for easy desserts. The recipes in this section are all about finding the easy way, whether that's just a simple concept, or finding a workaround and substituting some pre-bought elements, making it doable even for the busiest mums and dads to dish up dessert on a weeknight.

Finally, if the decadence of traditional desserts gets a bit much, or you just fancy something different, check out the Guilt-Free section of this book. Here you'll find recipes with a healthy twist, perhaps because they are low in sugar or dairy-free, or they include a 'superfood' ingredient such as chia seeds or matcha, or replace a some of the naughty stuff with good stuff – chocolate avocado mousse? Pumpkin doughnuts? Don't say no till you give it a go! You might be surprised how delicious they are.

CLASSIC

APPLE PIE AND CREAM

INGREDIENTS

Short crust pastry

2½ cups (310g, 10oz) plain flour

1 tbsp light brown sugar

¾ tsp salt

150g (5oz) chilled unsalted butter, cubed

⅓ cup (85g, 3oz) chilled Copha, cubed

⅓ cup (90ml, 3fl oz) chilled water

Filling

½ cup (110g, 4oz) caster sugar

¼ cup (40g, 1½ oz) packed light brown sugar

2 tbsps arrowroot flour

1 tbsp lemon juice

2 tsp finely grated orange zest

1 tsp allspice

1.2kg (2½ lbs) red apples (sundowner or pink lady), peeled, cored and cut into 1½ cm (¾ in) chunks

¼ cup (60ml, 2fl oz) milk, for brushing

2 tbsps sugar, for topping

2 cups (120g, 4oz) whipped cream, to serve

METHOD

1. Using a food processer, pulse together the flour, sugar and salt, gradually adding the butter and Copha until it resembles breadcrumbs. Gradually add the water until it comes together and can be formed into a single ball of dough. You may need less or more water, depending on the flour.

2. Knead it into a ball, then split it in two, making one slightly larger than the other, and form each half into a slightly flattened disc. Wrap each in plastic wrap, then place in the refrigerator to chill for at least 1 hour. You can make this at least 2 days ahead of time.

3. Preheat the oven to 200°C (400°F, Gas Mark 6) and grease a 23cm (9in) pie dish.

4. Roll out the larger piece of dough to 30cm (12in) in diameter. Transfer to the pie dish and let the edges hang over, then press into the side of the dish to form an rim. Brush the rim with a small amount of milk.

5. To make the filling, in a large bowl, gently mix together all the filling ingredients and combine thoroughly. Pour on top of the pastry in the pie dish.

6. Roll out the second disc of dough to about 30cm (12 in) diameter. Cut into 12 even-sized strips, about 2½ cm (1 in) wide. Place the strips across the top of the filling, making a lattice by weaving the strips over and under each other, and gently press into the edge of the pastry. Brush the pastry lattice with the milk and sprinkle the sugar over the top.

7. Bake for 10 minutes, then reduce heat to 190°C (375°F, Gas Mark 5). Bake for 1 hour 20 minutes or until the pastry is browned and the filling is bubbling. Cool on a wire rack for at least 1 hour. Serve with whipped cream.

SERVES 12 ★ PREP 2HR 30MIN ★ COOK TIME 45MIN

BLACK FOREST TRIFLE

INGREDIENTS

Cake

250g (9oz) unsalted butter

300g (10oz) brown sugar

2 large eggs, room temperature

1 tsp vanilla extract

120g (4oz) dark cooking chocolate, roughly chopped

160g (6oz) plain flour

1 tsp bicarbonate soda

Cherries

2 cups (200g, 7oz) fresh cherries, halved and pitted

1/3 cup (70g, 2½oz) caster sugar

1 tsp arrowroot flour

1/3 cup (80ml, 3fl oz) water

Cream filling

3 cups (750ml, 24fl oz) thickened cream

½ cup (110g, 4oz) caster sugar

½ tbsp vanilla paste

120g (4oz) dark chocolate, grated

1 cup (100g, 3½oz) fresh cherries, stems intact

METHOD

1. Preheat the oven to 190°C (375°F, Gas Mark 5) and grease a round cake tin.

2. Melt the chocolate in a heat-resistant bowl over a saucepan of gently simmering water. Set aside to cool.

3. Beat butter and sugar together until they resemble whipped cream. Add vanilla, then add in the eggs one at a time beating after each addition. Add the melted, slightly cooled chocolate and briefly mix through.

4. Sift the flour and baking soda together, then add the flour in thirds to the chocolate mix, combining well after each addition until a smooth batter forms.

5. Pour into the cake tin and bake for 20 minutes, then reduce the temperature to 160°C (325°F, Gas Mark 3) and bake for a further 25 minutes until a skewer inserted into the middle comes out clean. Let cool on a wire rack for at least 1 hour before using. Then cut the cake up into 3 x 4cm pieces, about 2cm thick.

6. Meanwhile, place the cherry halves, sugar, arrowroot flour and water in a medium saucepan and cook over medium-high heat until the liquid is nearly simmering. Remove from the heat and let cool for at least 30 minutes.

7. Whip the cream with the sugar and vanilla until soft peaks form.

8. Pour one third of the cream into the bottom of a serving bowl. Top with one half of the cherries in syrup along with one half of the cake slices. Sprinkle over one third of the grated chocolate. Repeat with a further third of the cream and chocolate and half the cherries. Top with remaining cream, then decorate with fresh cherries and dust with the remaining grated chocolate.

9. Refrigerate for at least 30 minutes before serving.

TIRAMISU

INGREDIENTS

2 large eggs, room temperature

⅓ cup (70g, 2½ oz) caster sugar

2½ cups (550ml, 20fl oz) espresso or very strong black coffee, cooled

460g (1lb) mascarpone cheese

400g (14oz) lady finger biscuits – crisp, not sponge

150g (5oz) plain dark chocolate, grated

2½ tbsps unsweetened cocoa powder

METHOD

1. Separate the eggs. In a medium bowl, whisk the egg yolks and sugar together until the mixture is thick, pale yellow, and forms a ribbon when the whisk is lifted out of the bowl, about 1 minute. Add ¼ cup coffee and the mascarpone and whisk until the mixture is smooth.

2. In a separate bowl, whisk the egg whites until soft peaks form when you lift the mixture out of the bowl. Gently fold the egg white into the mascarpone mixture.

3. Dip the biscuits, one at a time, into the remaining coffee; let them soak just long enough to become damp but not soggy.

4. Place one or two biscuits into the bottom of a large glass dish – enough to form a layer. Sprinkle over about half of the grated chocolate and layer over that around half of the mascarpone mixture. Repeat layering, then cover with plastic wrap and leave in the fridge until the mascarpone mixture is set, 8-10 hours or overnight.

5. When you are ready to serve, place the cocoa powder in a small sieve and dust over the top of the tiramisu.

CREME BRULEE

INGREDIENTS

4 cups (1L, 2pt) thickened cream

1 tsp vanilla extract

6 large egg yolks, room temperature

1 cup (220g, 8oz) caster sugar

8 cups (2L, 4pt) hot water

Fresh berries and sprigs of mint, to garnish

METHOD

1. Preheat the oven to 160°C (325°F, Gas Mark 3) and lightly oil six ramekins with a light oil such as vegetable or canola.

2. Place the cream and vanilla into a medium saucepan over medium-high heat and bring to a boil. Remove from the heat, cover with a tight-fitting lid and sit for 15 minutes.

3. Whisk together the egg yolks and half the sugar in a large mixing bowl until smooth and light in colour. Gradually add the cooled cream until completely mixed through.

4. Place a tea towel in the bottom of a large deep-sided baking dish and sit the ramekins on top. Fill the dish with enough hot water to come halfway up the sides of the ramekins.

5. Bake for 40 minutes or until the creme brulees are set. Remove them from the oven and let them sit for 1 hour, then place in the refrigerator to chill for at least 2 hours.

6. Just before serving, sprinkle the rest of the sugar over the top of each creme brulee. Use a kitchen torch to melt the sugar until it forms a slightly browned, crispy top. Serve garnished with mint and fresh berries.

KEY LIME PIE

INGREDIENTS

Pie crust

200g (7oz) Granita or other digestive biscuits

½ cup (125g, 4oz) butter, melted

½ cup (80g, 3oz) light brown sugar

Filling

1 x 400g (14oz) can sweetened condensed milk

5 egg yolks

½ cup (125ml, 4fl oz) thickened cream

½ cup (125ml, 4fl oz) fresh lime juice

1 tbsp finely grated lime zest (divided)

Slices of lime, to garnish

Topping

1 cup (250ml, 8fl oz) cream

½ cup (100g, 3½ oz) caster sugar

½ lime, finely sliced

METHOD

1. Preheat the oven to 190°C (375°F, Gas Mark 5) and line a 23cm (9in) springform cake tin with lightly greased baking paper.

2. Crush the biscuits by putting them in a plastic bag and bashing them with a rolling pin. You should end up with about 2 cups of crumbs.

3. Place all the crust ingredients together in a mixing bowl and mix thoroughly. Press the crumbs firmly into the bottom and about 4cm (1½ in) up the sides of the tin.

4. Line with foil and fill with baking beads and bake for 8 minutes. Place the shell on a wire rack to cool for at least 1 hour before adding the filling.

5. To make the filling, reduce the heat to 160°C (325°F, Gas Mark 3).

6. Add the condensed milk and egg yolks to a large bowl and whisk thoroughly until light and smooth.

7. Whisk in the cream and lime juice and 1 teaspoon of the lime zest. Pour into the pie crust and bake for 20 minutes. Set aside for at least 1 hour to cool before adding topping.

8. To make the topping, whip the cream until stiff peaks form, then beat in the sugar. Spoon the cream mixture around the edge of the pie, sprinkle the leftover zest on top and garnish with twisted slices of lime.

CHOCOLATE FONDANT

INGREDIENTS

100g (3½ oz) unsalted butter, plus extra to grease

¼ cup (30g, 1oz) cacao powder

100g (3½ oz) dark cooking chocolate (70% cocoa solids or highter), chopped

2 large eggs, room temperature

2 large egg yolks, room temperature

²/₃ cup (120g, 4oz) caster sugar

½ tsp vanilla extract

²/₃ cup (80g, 3oz) plain flour

1 cup (125g, 4oz) fresh berries

6 small sprigs of mint, to garnish

METHOD

1. Preheat the oven to 180°C (350°F, Gas Mark 4) and liberally grease six small individual pudding ramekins or dariole moulds with butter. Then dust with cacao powder.

2. In a small bowl set over a saucepan of hot water, slowly melt the chocolate and butter. Remove bowl from heat and stir until smooth – try not to stir too much as it makes the filling less glossy. Let cool for 10 minutes.

3. Beat the eggs, yolks, sugar and vanilla extract together until pale and thickened. Use a whisk or slotted spoon to fold in the melted chocolate. Sift the flour over the mixture and again fold in to combine.

4. Divide the batter between the ramekins and bake for 12 minutes.

5. Very carefully loosen the puddings from the moulds so as not to break the cake part. Set them upside down on serving plates. Dust lightly with remaining cacao powder and top with berries and a sprig of mint.

RICE PUDDING

INGREDIENTS

4 cups (1L, 2pt) milk

¾ cup (165g, 6oz) short-grain rice

¼ tsp salt

½ cup (110g, 4oz) caster sugar

½ tsp vanilla extract

½ tsp allspice

½ tsp ground nutmeg

METHOD

1. Place the milk, rice and salt in a large saucepan over medium-high heat and bring to the boil. Reduce heat to low and cook, stirring, for 30 minutes or until the rice is tender.

2. Add the sugar, vanilla and allspice. Increase heat to medium-high and bring to the boil. Boil for a further 2 minutes or until the rice is soft and the mixture thickens.

3. Spoon the rice evenly among serving bowls. Sprinkle with nutmeg and serve warm.

PECAN PIE

INGREDIENTS

Pastry

1¼ cups (175g, 6oz) plain flour

½ tsp salt

1 tbsp caster sugar

115g (4oz) unsalted butter, chilled, cut into 2cm (1in) cubes

¼ cup (60ml, 2fl oz) ice water

Filling

1½ cups (185g, 6oz) pecans

1¼ cups (210g, 7oz) dark brown sugar

²/₃ cup (230g, 8oz) golden syrup

1 tbsp bourbon

60g (2oz) unsalted butter, room temperature

3 large eggs, room temperature

¼ cup (60ml, 2fl oz) thickened cream

½ tsp vanilla extract

¼ tsp salt

METHOD

1. Using a food processer, pulse together the flour, salt, sugar and butter together until it resembles breadcrumbs. Gradually add the water until it comes together and can be formed into a single ball of dough. You may need less or more water, depending on the flour. Knead for 4 minutes then form into a slightly flattened disc. Wrap in plastic wrap, then place in the refrigerator to chill for at least 30 minutes.

2. Grease a fluted 23cm (9in) pie dish. Roll out the dough onto a lightly floured surface into a roughly 33cm (12½ in) circle. Transfer to the pie dish. Tuck any overhanging pastry back under itself. Let chill for at least 30 minutes before filling.

3. Preheat the oven to 180°C (350°F, Gas Mark 4) and line a large flat baking tray with baking paper. Scatter the pecans on top in one layer and bake for 10 minutes or until lightly browned. Let cool, reserve 6 pecans and chop the rest.

4. In a large saucepan, heat the brown sugar, syrup, bourbon and butter until boiling, stirring all the while. Remove from heat and let cool for 30 minutes. In a separate large mixing bowl, briskly whisk the eggs. Mix the cooled sugar mixture into the eggs, along with the chopped pecans, cream, vanilla and salt.

5. Pour the filling into the pastry case. Arrange the reserved pecans on top for decoration. Bake for about 45 to 50 minutes, or until a skewer inserted in the middle comes out clean. Remove from oven and place on a wire rack to cool. Serve warm or at room temperature with whipping cream.

CREME CARAMEL

INGREDIENTS

Caramel

1¼ cups (195g, 7oz) light brown sugar

⅓ cup (80ml, 3fl oz) water

Custard

1½ cups (375ml, 13fl oz) whole milk

1½ cups (375ml, 13fl oz) light cream

6 medium eggs

⅔ cup (140g, 5oz) caster sugar

½ tsp vanilla extract

¼ tsp ground cinnamon

Pinch of table salt

8 sprigs of mint, to garnish

METHOD

1. Preheat the oven to 180°C (350°F, Gas Mark 4). Heat sugar and water in a saucepan over medium heat for 8 minutes or until syrup begins to turn golden. Immediately remove from the heat and pour even amounts of syrup into the bottom of eight ramekins or dariole moulds. Swirl the syrup to ensure even coating. Set aside.

2. Heat milk and cream in a saucepan over medium heat for 5 minutes until just below boiling. Pour into a bowl, set aside to cool. Lightly whisk eggs in a separate bowl, then beat in sugar, vanilla extract, cinnamon and salt. Slowly mix into the cream. Strain the mixture into the ramekins.

3. Place a tea towel in the bottom of a large roasting dish and stand the ramekins on top of the towel. Pour boiling water into the pan until it comes halfway up the sides of the ramekins. Place in the oven. Bake for 40 minutes. Transfer ramekins to a wire rack to cool. Then chill in a refrigerator for at least 2 hours.

4. To serve, run a round-edged knife around the side of the ramekins, pushing away from the custard. Hold serving plate upside down over the top of the ramekin and quickly flip the plate and ramekin over. Garnish with mint.

SALTED CARAMEL CREAM

INGREDIENTS

2 cups (310g, 10oz) light brown sugar

175g (6oz) unsalted butter, room temperature, roughly chopped

¾ cup (185ml, 6fl oz) thickened cream, room temperature

1 tbsp non-iodised salt

METHOD

1. Heat the sugar in a heavy medium saucepan over medium-high heat until it just starts to melt. Immediately begin stirring it briskly until all melted. Let it cook until it begins to turn golden. As soon as it does, whisk in the butter gradually.

2. Remove from the heat briefly if it looks like turning a darker-than-golden colour. Do not let it burn!

3. Once all the butter is stirred in, remove the pot from the heat and gradually add the cream. Stir until thickened and smooth.

4. Add the salt and stir through.

5. Let the sauce cool for at least 30 minutes before use.

   Note: Will keep in a sealed container in the fridge for up to 4 weeks.

CHOCOLATE SOUFFLE

INGREDIENTS

⅓ cup (95g, 3oz) caster sugar

150g (5oz) dark cooking chocolate, roughly chopped

2 large egg yolks, separated, room temperature

2 tbsps thickened cream

2 tsps plain flour

¼ tsp ground allspice

6 large egg whites, room temperature

¼ tsp salt

2 tbsps icing sugar, for dusting

METHOD

1. Preheat the oven to 190°C (375°F, Gas Mark 5) and position rack in centre of oven.

2. Grease four ramekins with butter and then dust with about 2 tablespoons of the caster sugar.

3. Melt the chocolate in a double boiler. Once it is almost melted, remove it from the heat and let it melt completely on its own.

4. Whisk the yolks and cream together in a large mixing bowl. Add the chocolate and whisk until smooth. Add the flour and allspice and mix until completely incorporated.

5. In a separate bowl, beat the egg whites and salt together until soft peaks form. Whisk in the rest of the sugar until the whites become glossy and form stiff peaks. Use a slotted spoon to gently fold in half the egg whites into the chocolate mixture. Then gently fold the chocolate mixture into the remaining egg white mixture until completely incorporated.

6. Divide the mix between the four ramekins and bake for 17 minutes. The souffles should have risen by about two thirds of their original height and be set on top.

7. Dust with icing sugar and serve warm.

BAKED APPLES

INGREDIENTS

⅔ cup (100g, 3oz) light brown sugar

½ tbsp allspice

⅔ cup (100g, 3½ oz) sultanas

½ cup (60g, 2oz) chopped walnuts

6 large red apples, (sundowner or pink lady), cored

2 tbsps butter

Ice cream, to serve

METHOD

1. Preheat the oven to 180°C (350°F, Gas Mark 4) and line a deep baking tray big enough to hold the 6 apples with baking paper.

2. In a medium mixing bowl, toss together the sugar, allspice, sultanas and walnuts.

3. Spoon the mixture evenly and firmly into the middle of the cored apples.

4. Place a small amount of butter on the top of each apple and place them in the baking tray.

5. Bake for 50 minutes until the apples are soft and cooked through. Let sit for 10 minutes before serving with ice cream.

STICKY DATE PUDDING

INGREDIENTS

Puddings

1¾ cups (305g, 10oz) Medjool dates, pitted and chopped

1 tsp bicarbonate of soda

1½ cups (375ml, 13fl oz) boiling water

85g (3oz) unsalted butter, room temperature

¾ cup (165g, 6oz) caster sugar

2 eggs, room temperature

1 cup (125g, 4oz) self-raising flour

Sauce

¾ cup (125g, 4oz) packed light brown sugar

²/₃ cup (160ml, 5fl oz) thickened cream

75g (3oz) butter

½ tsp vanilla extract

METHOD

1. Preheat the oven to 180°C (350°F, Gas Mark 4) and grease 10 ramekins or dariole moulds.

2. Place the dates and bicarbonate of soda in a small bowl and pour enough boiling water over to cover them.

3. Whisk the butter and caster sugar together until it resembles whipped cream. Beat in the eggs, one add a time, mixing in thoroughly before adding the next.

4. Sift the flour into the mixture in thirds and then stir through the date mixture. Pour into the ramekins.

5. Bake for 15-20 minutes or until a skewer inserted in the middle comes out clean.

6. In a medium saucepan, add the sauce ingredients and stir over medium-high heat until boiling. Turn down to a simmer and cook for 5 minutes.

7. Serve the puddings with the hot sauce poured over the top.

NEW YORK CHEESECAKE

INGREDIENTS

Base

10 Granita biscuits, crushed

2 tbsps brown sugar

75g (3oz) unsalted butter, melted

Filling

1.2kg (2½ lbs) cream cheese, at room temperature, cubed

1½ cups (330g, 12oz) caster sugar

¼ tsp salt

⅓ cup (80g, 3oz) creme fraiche

1½ tsps lemon juice

1 tsp finely grated lemon zest

2 tsps vanilla extract

2 egg yolks, room temperature

6 eggs, room temperature

1 cup (125g, 4oz) mixed fresh berries, to garnish

½ cup (80g, 3oz) white chocolate buttons, to garnish

Sprigs of mint, to garnish

METHOD

1. To make the base, preheat the oven to 150°C (300°F, Gas Mark 2) and grease a 23cm (9in) springform cake tin. Line the bottom only with baking paper.

2. Mix together all the base ingredients and stir to combine thoroughly. Press into the bottom of the cake tin. Bake for 15 minutes in the lower part of the oven. Set aside to cool while making the filling.

3. Increase the oven temperature to 250°C (490°F, Gas Mark 10). Beat the cream cheese on medium-low speed for 1 minute. Beat in half the sugar and the salt and beat on medium-low speed for another 1 minute. Scrape down the bowl as needed while mixing in this stage. Add the rest of the sugar and beat until mixed through completely. Mix in the creme fraiche, lemon juice, zest and vanilla. Mix through for 1 minute. Add the egg yolks and ensure they're thoroughly combined. Add the eggs, ensuring each is mixed through before adding the next.

4. Pour the filling into the cake tin and bake for 10 minutes. Turn the oven down to 100°C (200°F) and bake for 1 hour 30 minutes.

5. Let the cake cool in the tin for 5 minutes before running a thin spatula or knife around the edge, then let sit for at least 3 hours in the refrigerator.

6. Again run a spatula around the edge before loosening the tin. Slide the cake out onto a serving plate.

7. Serve decorated with berries, chocolate buttons and mint sprigs.

PEAR GALETTE

INGREDIENTS

1¾ (215g, 7oz) cups plain flour

⅓ cup (70g, 2½ oz) caster sugar

¼ cup (15g, ½ oz) fine polenta

¼ tsp salt

120g (4oz) unsalted butter, chilled and chopped into 1cm (½ in) cubes

⅓ cup (80ml, 3fl oz) milk

4 medium Buerre Bosc pears, peeled, cored, halved and thinly sliced

1 tsp cinnamon

½ tbsp orange juice

1 egg, lightly beaten

1 tbsp water

2 tbsps raw sugar

METHOD

1. To make the dough, use a food processor to pulse the flour, sugar, polenta, salt and butter a few times until it resembles breadcrumbs. Add the milk a small amount at a time and process until it comes together to form a ball. Knead for 4 minutes then form into a slightly flattened disc. Wrap in plastic wrap, then place in the refrigerator to chill for at least 1 hour.

2. Preheat the oven to 180°C (350°F, Gas Mark 4) and line a baking tray with lightly greased baking paper.

3. Roll out the dough on a lightly floured surface to form a 36cm (14in) circle. Transfer to the baking tray.

4. Gently toss the pears with the cinnamon and orange juice. Arrange the pears in a spiral pattern from the outside in, leaving a 5cm (2in) border all around. Gently fold the edge over the pears and crimp the edges with a fork.

5. Mix the egg and water together and brush the edge of the pastry with the egg wash. Sprinkle the sugar over the top and bake for 45 minutes. Serve warm.

PEACH COBBLER

INGREDIENTS

Filling

⅓ cup (70g, 2½ oz) caster sugar

1 tbsp arrowroot flour

½ tsp allspice

8 peaches (preferably clingstone), sliced

2 tbsps water

2 tsps lemon juice

Topping

1½ cups (185g, 6oz) plain flour

2 tsps baking powder

½ tsp salt

225g (½ lb) unsalted butter, chilled and chopped into 1cm (½ in) cubes

¾ cup (185ml, 6fl oz) thickened cream, plus more for brushing

1 tbsp sugar

METHOD

1. Preheat the oven to 200°C (400°F, Gas Mark 6).

2. Mix together all the filling ingredients in a large saucepan and heat until boiling. Reduce the heat to low and gently stir for 1 minute. Remove from heat and pour into a large baking dish.

3. Using a food processer, pulse together the flour, baking powder, salt and butter until it resembles breadcrumbs. Stir in the cream until a soft dough forms.

4. Drop large spoonfulls of the dough onto the peach mixture. Sprinkle the sugar over the top.

5. Bake for 25 minutes or until the top is browned.

6. Serve hot with ice cream or cream.

SERVES 8 ★ PREP 1HR (PLUS CHILLING) ★ COOK TIME 30MIN

LEMON MERINGUE PIE

INGREDIENTS

Pastry

1½ cups (185g, 6oz) flour

½ cup (110g, 4oz) caster sugar

Pinch of salt

125g (4oz) unsalted butter, softened

2 egg yolks, room temperature, lightly beaten

1½ tbsps chilled water

Filling

1½ cups (330g, 12oz) caster sugar

2 cups (500ml, 1pt) water

½ cup (70g, 2½ oz) arrowroot flour

120g (4oz) unsalted butter, chopped

Pinch of salt

7 large egg yolks, room temperature

¾ cup (175ml, 6fl oz) lemon juice

2 tsps lemon zest

Meringue

3 egg whites

1 cup (220g, 8oz) caster sugar

½ tsp arrowroot flour

1 tbsp water

METHOD

1. Using a food processer, pulse together the flour, sugar, salt and butter until it resembles breadcrumbs. Mix in the egg yolks then gradually add the water until it forms a ball. You may need less or more water, depending on the flour. Knead for 4 minutes then form into a slightly flattened disc. Wrap in plastic wrap, then place in the refrigerator to chill for at least 30 minutes.

2. Preheat the oven to 180°C (350°F, Gas Mark 4) and grease a 20cm (8in) round pie dish.

3. Roll out the dough on a lightly floured surface into a 25cm (10in) round circle. Place in the pie dish and press against the sides. Trim off any overhang. Very lightly prick the base with a fork. Place a sheet of foil over the pastry and fill with baking beads or dried beans. Blind bake for 10 minutes, then remove the beads and foil. Bake for another 10 minutes then set aside to cool.

4. To make the filling, place the sugar and half the water in a large saucepan and bring to the boil. Reduce heat to low. Mix together the arrowroot flour and remaining water in a small bowl. Slowly add the flour mix to the saucepan and whisk in thoroughly. Add butter and salt and stir until melted through.

5. Place a quarter of a cup of the warm sugar mixture into a medium bowl with the egg yolks, lemon juice and zest and mix thoroughly. Slowly add the yolk mixture into the saucepan. Turn the heat up to high and stir continuously until thickened and almost boiling. Then pour into the pastry case. Place in the refrigerator for up to 2 hours to chill and set.

6. Preheat the oven again to 180°C (350°F, Gas Mark 4). To make the meringue, whisk the egg whites until firm peaks form. Gradually add in the sugar, flour and water a quarter at a time until the sugar is completely dissolved into the meringue. Spoon the meringue over the filling and bake for 5 minutes until the top of the meringue starts to brown. Let cool before serving.

BREAD AND BUTTER PUDDING

INGREDIENTS

3 large eggs, plus 1 yolk, room temperature

3 tbsps light brown sugar

1 cup (250ml, 8fl oz) milk

1¼ cups (300ml, 10fl oz) thickened cream

1 tsp vanilla extract

½ tsp ground cinnamon

½ tsp allspice

8 large, thick slices of day-old white sourdough

50g (2oz) reduced-salt butter, room temperature

⅔ cup (100g, 3½ oz) sultanas

1 tbsp orange zest

2 tbsps raw sugar

METHOD

1. Whisk together the eggs, yolk and brown sugar in a medium mixing bowl.

2. Heat the milk, cream, vanilla, cinnamon and allspice in a large saucepan over medium-high heat until almost about to boil. Reduce the heat to low and gradually pour the egg mixture into the saucepan, stirring all the while until smooth and thickened slightly.

3. Grease a deep-sided baking dish. Cut the crusts off the bread, butter both sides of each slice and cut into quarters diagonally. Arrange half the bread, slightly overlapping each triangle, in the bottom of the dish. Spread half the sultanas and zest over the top. Repeat with the rest of the bread and fruit.

4. Pour the egg mixture over the top and let it soak in for at least 40 minutes in the refrigerator.

5. Preheat the oven to 180°C (350°F, Gas Mark 4). Sprinkle the raw sugar over the top just before baking and bake in the oven for 40 minutes until golden and the custard is mostly set.

6. Serve warm with ice cream or cream.

TARTE TATIN

INGREDIENTS

⅔ cup (100g, 3oz) light brown sugar

½ tsp ground cinnamon
60g (2oz) unsalted butter, chilled and chopped

900g (2lb) dessert apples such as royal gala or Fuji, peeled, quartered and cored

25g (1oz) unsalted butter, melted

300g (10oz) butter puff pastry sheets

METHOD

1. Preheat the oven to 180°C (350°F, Gas Mark 4).

2. Sprinkle the sugar and cinnamon over the bottom of a 20cm (8in) round flame-proof baking dish or oven-proof frying pan. Heat over medium-heat for 7 mins until the sugar begins to turn golden brown and is just starting to smoke. Remove from the heat and stir in the chilled butter.

3. Arrange the apples in a snug circle around the edge of the dish, cut side up. Arrange them in concentric circles to fill the dish. Make sure the apples are sitting snugly with no gaps. Brush the top of the apples with the melted butter. Bake for 30 minutes then remove from the oven.

4. Cut the puff pastry into a 24cm (9½ in) circle and prick lightly with a fork. Place over the top of the dish, tucking the edges into the inside of the dish.

5. Bake for 40 minutes or until the pastry is golden brown and crisped. Allow to cool to room temperature. To serve, run a knife around the edge of the dish and invert onto a large serving plate.

PROFITEROLES

INGREDIENTS

Choux pastry

¾ cup (200ml, 7fl oz) filtered water

4 tsps caster sugar

85g (3oz) unsalted butter, room temperature

1 cup (115g, 4oz) plain flour

Pinch of salt

3 medium eggs, lightly beaten

Filling

2 cups (500ml, 1pt) thickened cream

2 tbsps orange zest

To serve

1 portion chocolate sauce (see recipe page 16)

¼ cup (30g, 1oz) dry-roasted hazelnuts, roughly chopped

METHOD

1. Preheat the oven to 200°C (400°F, Gas Mark 6) and lightly grease a large baking tray.

2. To make the choux pastry, heat the water, sugar and butter in a large saucepan over medium heat until the butter is melted and combined. Increase the heat to high, then tip the flour and salt in and stir vigorously until you have a smooth paste. Keep cooking until it starts to come away from the sides. Remove the mixture from the saucepan into a mixing bowl and let cool for 10 minutes.

3. Beat in the eggs, a third at a time, until the mixture forms a glossy dough. The mixture should drop away from the spoon. use two dessertspoons to form round balls of dough on the baking sheet about 4cm (1½ in) apart. (You should get 18 or more balls.) Brush a very small amount of water on each ball and place the tray in the oven. At the same time place a shallow ovenproof dish half-filled with water in the bottom of the oven.

4. Bake the profiteroles for 25 minutes until golden brown and puffed. Remove from the oven and poke a hole in the base of each with a skewer. Return them to the tray with the base facing upwards and bake for another 5 minutes. Leave to cool completely on the tray while you prepare the filling.

5. Whip the cream with the orange zest. Once the profiteroles have cooled, pipe the filling into the middle of each.

6. Heat the chocolate sauce and add the hazelnuts to it. Serve each profiterole drizzled with the chocolate hazelnut sauce.

FRUIT CRUMBLE

INGREDIENTS

Crumble

140g (5oz) unsalted butter, chilled, cut into 1cm (½ in) cubes

¾ cup (120g, 4oz) firmly packed brown sugar

1 cup (125g, 4oz) plain flour

1½ cups (130g, 4½ oz) rolled oats

Filling

1 cup (200g, 7oz) strawberries, hulled and chopped

1¾ cups (200g, 7oz) raspberries, fresh or frozen

2 cups (200g, 7oz) blueberries

200g (7oz) rhubarb, cut into 1½ cm (¾ in) pieces

1 tsp vanilla extract

4 tbsps brown sugar

1 tsp finely grated lemon zest

1 tsp ground cinnamon

½ tsp ground cardamom

METHOD

1. Preheat the oven to 180°C (350°F, Gas Mark 4).

2. In a food processer, pulse the crumble ingredients together a few times to combine and make a loose mixture. Remove to a large mixing bowl and use your fingers to press it together to make larger chunks. (Crumble will keep in a sealed container in the freezer up to 2 months)

3. Combine the filling ingredients in a large mixing bowl and gently stir to coat the fruit in the sugar and spices.

4. Place the fruit in the bottom of a deep baking dish. Top with the crumble.

5. Bake for 50 minutes or until the fruit is softened and the crumble is golden brown.

6. Serve warm with ice cream, cream or custard.

STICKY POACHED PEARS

INGREDIENTS

1 cup (250ml, 8fl oz) white wine (such as pinot grigio)

4 star anise

1 vanilla pod

2 large pears (Buerre Bosc), halved, core removed, stems intact

1 tbsp honey

1 tsp ground cinnamon

METHOD

1. Place the wine, star anise and vanilla pod in a medium saucepan over high heat and bring to a boil. Reduce the heat and bring to a simmer.

2. Add the pears and simmer, covered, for 10 minutes, turning halfway. Remove from the saucepan and keep warm while reducing the sauce

3. Bring the liquid to a boil again and stir in the honey. Reduce to a simmer and cook for 5 minutes until thickened to a syrup.

4. Remove the vanilla pod and star anise.

5. Serve the pear halves warm and drizzled in syrup.

CHURROS CON CHOCOLAT

INGREDIENTS

1 portion chocolate sauce
(see recipe page 16)

1 tsp cinnamon

¼ tsp cayenne pepper

Churros

3 cups (375g, 12oz) plain
flour

1 tsp baking powder

1 tsp cinnamon

1 tsp salt

2½ cups (625ml, 20fl oz)
water

2 tbsps light brown sugar

2 egg yolks

Canola oil, for frying

½ cup (110g, 4oz) sugar
for dusting

METHOD

1. Heat the chocolate sauce and stir in the cinnamon and cayenne pepper. Set aside but keep warm.

2. To make the churros, sift the flour, baking powder, cinnamon and salt into a large mixing bowl. Make a well in the centre.

3. Heat the water in a small saucepan until boiling. Reduce the heat to a simmer and add the brown sugar and stir until the sugar is dissolved. Pour into the flour mix. Whisk until the mixture is fluffy and smooth. Add the egg yolks one at a time and keep whisking until the batter is shiny.

4. Fill a pastry bag, fitted with a star-shaped nozzle if you have one, with the mixture.

5. Heat 5cm (2in) (2in) of oil in a large deep-sided frying pan over high heat. If you have a thermometer, heat to 190°C (375°F).

6. Pipe 10cm (4in) lengths of churro batter into the hot oil, using a knife to cut off the lengths.

7. Fry for 3-4 minutes until golden brown. Place on a wire rack with paper towels underneath to drain. Sprinkle with the sugar and serve warm with the chocolate dipping sauce.

Note: Use a cloth or heavy duty-plastic bag to pipe. A Ziploc bag isn't strong enough to cope with the weight of the batter.

CHERRY PIE

INGREDIENTS

Crust

2 cups (250g, 8oz) plain flour, sifted

½ tsp cooking salt

1 tbsp caster sugar

180g (6oz) unsalted butter, chilled and cut into cubes

⅓ cup (80ml, 3fl oz) chilled water

Cherry filling

4 cups (800g, 1¾ lb) fresh cherries, pitted (can also use bottled or tinned)

⅓ cup (80ml, 3fl oz) cherry juice

¾ cup (150g, 5oz) caster sugar

¼ cup (30g, 1oz) arrowroot flour

Pinch of salt

1 tbsp lemon juice

½ tsp almond extract

25g (1oz) unsalted butter, cubed

2 tbsps milk

METHOD

1. Add the flour, salt, sugar and butter to a food processor and pulse until the mixture resembles breadcrumbs. Add half the water and mix through, then slowly add the rest until the mixture starts to come together in a dough.

2. Form the dough into a flattened disc and wrap in plastic wrap. Place in the refrigerator for at least 30 minutes to chill. In the meantime, grease a 23cm (9in) pie dish and set aside.

3. Roll out the dough on a lightly floured work surface and roll into a 30cm (12in) circle. Gently transfer to the pie dish. Prick the bottom very lightly with a fork and crimp the edges. Set aside.

4. Preheat the oven to 220°C (425°F, Gas Mark 7).

5. In a large mixing bowl, toss the cherries together with the cherry juice, sugar, arrowroot, salt, lemon juice and almond extract until thoroughly combined. Pour into the pie shell and dot with the pieces of butter. Lightly brush the edge of the pastry with milk.

7. Bake in the oven for 15 minutes, then reduce the temperature to 180°C (350°F, Gas Mark 4) and bake for 20 minutes or until the crust is golden. Cool on a wire rack for at least 3 hours.

TREACLE SPONGE PUDDING

INGREDIENTS

175g (6oz) unsalted butter, room temperature

1¼ cups (175g, 6oz) light brown sugar

2 tbsps lemon zest

3 medium eggs, lightly beaten, room temperature

2½ cups (300g, 10oz) plain flour

2 tsps baking powder

2 tbsps full cream milk

⅓ cup (115g, 4oz) treacle (substitute golden syrup, if desired)

METHOD

1. Grease a large heatproof pudding basin and line with baking paper.

2. Beat the butter, sugar and lemon zest together until pale. Add the eggs and mix through thoroughly.

3. Sift together the flour and baking powder. Add to the butter mixture, a third at a time until incorporated, then beat through the milk.

4. Pour the treacle into the basin and pour the batter over the top. Cover with a circle of baking paper and then a layer of foil. Secure with clips or strings.

5. Place the basin a large pot and pour in enough boiling water to come halfway up the sides. Bring to the boil, then simmer, covered, for 2 hours.

6. Let the pudding cool for 10 minutes before inverting onto a large serving plate and carefully removing the paper.

7. Serve with custard or cream and an extra drizzle of treacle.

LEMON TART

INGREDIENTS

Pastry

2½ cups (300g, 10oz) plain flour

150g (5oz) cold unsalted butter, chopped

1 large egg, room temperature

¼ cup (60ml, 2fl oz) cold water

Lemon filling

6 large eggs

1¼ cup (250g, 9oz) caster sugar

2 medium lemons, zest finely grated

¾ cup (185ml, 6fl oz) lemon juice, strained

¾ cup (200ml, 7fl oz) thickened cream

¼ cup (10g, ¼ oz) loosely packed thin lemon zest strips

Icing sugar, for dusting

METHOD

1. Using a food processor, pulse together the flour and butter until it resembles breadcrumbs. Mix in the egg then gradually add the water until it comes together and can be formed into a single ball of dough. You may need less or more water, depending on the flour. Knead for 4 minutes then form into a slightly flattened disc. Wrap in plastic wrap, then place in the refrigerator to chill for at least 30 minutes. You can make this at least 2 days ahead of time.

2. Preheat the oven to 200°C (400°F, Gas Mark 6) and grease a 25cm (10in) loose-bottom fluted tart tin.

3. Roll out pastry to 3mm (⅛ in) thickness on a lightly floured work surface, then remove to the tin and trim off any excess pastry around the edge. Lightly prick the bottom, line with foil or baking paper and then fill with baking beads or dried beans.

4. Blind bake for 15 minutes until pastry is dry. Remove the foil and beads and return to the oven for a further 15 minutes. Remove from oven and set aside to cool completely.

5. Reduce oven to 160°C (325°F, Gas Mark 3).

6. To make the filling, whisk together the eggs and sugar in a large mixing bowl until pale and creamy. Stir in the lemon zest, juice and cream, mixing well to combine.

7. Place the tart case onto a large baking tray and fill with the lemon curd. Sprinkle the strips of lemon zest on top of the curd.Bake for 35 minutes or until just set.

8. Remove from oven and let cool for at least 1 hour or until the filling is firm. Dust with icing sugar before serving.

BANOFFEE PIE

INGREDIENTS

Base

1 packet ginger snap biscuits

200g (7oz) butter, melted

Toffee

1 cup (200g, 7oz) caster sugar

¼ cup (50ml, 2fl oz) water

80g (3oz) butter, roughly chopped

½ cup (125ml, 4fl oz) whipping cream

Pinch of salt

Topping

6 ripe bananas, thinly sliced (reserve 8 slices for garnish)

1⅔ cups (400ml, 13fl oz) whipping cream

¾ cup (200ml, 7fl oz) sour cream

1 tbsp vanilla extract

8 sprigs of mint

⅓ cup (50g, 2oz) dark chocolate, shaved

3 tbsps white chocolate, shaved

METHOD

1. Process the biscuits in a food processor until they become fine crumbs and remove to a mixing bowl. Stir through the butter and press the mix into the base and sides of a 24cm (9½ in) springform cake tin. Place in the refrigerator for at least 2 hours to set.

2. Place the sugar and water in a medium saucepan over medium heat. Stir until the sugar has dissolved, then bring to the boil and cook until it begins to turn golden. Immediately stir in the butter and cream and a pinch of salt. Bring to the boil, then reduce heat and simmer for 10 minutes until thickened.

3. Pour the toffee filling over the base, then refrigerate for at least 2 hours to set.

4. Arrange the banana slices on top of the caramel.

5. Whip the cream, sour cream and vanilla together until stiff peaks form. Spoon over the banana slices. Decorate with reserved banana slices and mint sprigs, then sprinkle the grated chocolate over the top. Serve chilled.

SERVES 6 ★ PREP 30MIN (PLUS CHILLING) ★ COOK TIME 10MIN

DARK CHOCOLATE MOUSSE

INGREDIENTS

240g (4oz) dark cooking chocolate (try to use a good quality brand)

60g (2oz) unsalted butter

4 large eggs, separated

¼ tsp cream of tartar

½ cup (120g, 4oz) caster sugar

1⅔ cups (400ml, 13fl oz) thickened cream

½ tsp vanilla extract

6 sprigs of mint, to garnish

1 tbsp cocoa powder

METHOD

1. Melt chocolate and butter in a heat-resistant bowl over a saucepan of gently simmering water. Remove from the heat and gently whisk in the egg yolks. Set aside to cool for at least 30 minutes.

2. Beat the egg whites with the cream of tartar and 4 tablespoons of the sugar until stiff peaks form.

3. In a separate bowl, whisk the cream with the vanilla extract and the remaining sugar until soft peaks form. Set aside about one third of the cream for serving.

4. Use a slotted spoon to gently fold a third of the egg whites into the cooled chocolate mixture. Repeat the same with the whipped cream. Continue until the egg whites and whipped cream are all incorporated into the chocolate. The consistency should be smooth, light and creamy.

5. Chill in the fridge for at least 2 hours before serving. Serve with a dollop of the reserved whipped cream, a sprig of mint and sprinkled with cocoa powder.

ITALIAN CANNOLI

INGREDIENTS

Shells

2 cups (250g, 8oz) plain flour

2 tbsps unsalted butter, room temperature

1 tsp caster sugar

½ tsp ground cinnamon

Pinch of salt

¾ cup (185ml, 6fl oz) Marsala or sweet sherry

1 egg white, lightly beaten

½ cup (125ml, 4fl oz) olive (or canola) oil

Filling

3 cups fresh ricotta cheese (not from a container)

½ cup (80g, 3oz) icing sugar, plus extra for dusting

½ tsp vanilla extract

½ cup (80g, 3oz) high-quality chocolate, coarsely grated (optional)

½ cup (60g, 2oz) pistachios, finely chopped

METHOD

1. To make the shells, beat together the flour, butter, sugar, cinnamon and salt. Slowly add the Marsala, until the dough comes together to form a firm ball.

2. Knead for 3 minutes until smooth, then form into a slightly flattened disc, wrap in plastic wrap and set aside for 1 hour.

3. Halve the dough, then roll out on a lightly floured board to 5mm (¼ in) thick.

4. Cut into four rounds about 10cm (4in) in diameter and place a lightly oiled round metal cannoli tube at one end. Roll the dough around the tube and seal the edges with egg white.

5. Heat the oil in a medium saucepan until it reaches 190°C (375°F).

6. Drop one or two tubes into the hot oil at one time, and cook until golden. Carefully remove from the pan, cool, and gently slide the cannoli shell from the tube. Repeat with the rest of the dough.

7. To make the filling, sit the ricotta in a strainer to remove excess liquid. Mix the ricotta in a large bowl with the sugar, vanilla and chocolate. Cover the bowl and chill in the refrigerator for 30 minutes.

8. Use a large piping bag to fill the shells with the ricotta mixture. Scatter the pistachios in a small shallow bowl and gently press each end of the cannolis into the bowl to coat in pistachios. Dust tops with extra icing sugar.

ETON MESS

INGREDIENTS

1 cup (125g, 4oz) fresh or frozen raspberries

¼ cup (55g, 2oz) caster sugar

1¼ cups (300ml, 10fl oz) whipping cream

¼ tsp vanilla extract

4 small meringues

2¼ cups (450g, 1lb) strawberries, hulled and chopped, reserve 2 whole strawberries for garnish

Mint leaves, to garnish

METHOD

1. Add the raspberries and sugar to a small saucepan over low heat for 8 minutes until the raspberries start to break apart. Remove from heat and set aside for 30 minutes to cool.

2. Puree the raspberries with a blender until you have a smooth puree. Press the puree through a sieve to remove the seeds and any solids.

3. Whip the cream with the vanilla extract until stiff peaks form. Crumble the meringues and add to a large mixing bowl with the whipped cream, raspberry puree and chopped strawberries. Mix thoroughly.

4. Serve the mess garnished with sliced strawberries and a mint leaf.

VANILLA PUDDING

INGREDIENTS

1½ gold-strength gelatine leaves

1½ tbsps full cream milk

¾ cup (200ml, 7fl oz) thickened cream

1 tsp strained orange juice

½ tsp vanilla extract

¼ cup (35g, 1¼ oz) caster sugar

Strawberries, to garnish

Sprigs of mint, to garnish

METHOD

1. Soak the gelatine leaves in a bowl of cold water for 5 minutes.

2. Place the milk, half the cream, orange juice and vanilla in a small saucepan over medium-high heat and bring to a boil. Reduce heat and gently simmer for 6 minutes.

3. Squeeze the liquid from the gelatine leaves and whisk the leaves into the cream mixture. Set aside to cool for 30 minutes.

4. Whip the rest of the cream with the sugar until stiff peaks form. Use a slotted spoon to fold this into the cooled cream mixture.

5. Pour into two lightly oiled (use canola or vegetable oil) individual dessert moulds and chill in the refrigerator for at least 3 hours to set.

6. To serve briefly dip the moulds in hot water, then turn out onto serving plates. Garnish with strawberries and mint.

ENGLISH TRIFLE

INGREDIENTS

Custard

1½ cups (375ml, 13fl oz) milk

1 cup (250ml, 8fl oz) thickened cream

½ tsp vanilla extract

6 medium egg yolks

½ cup (110g, 4oz) caster sugar

2 tsps arrowroot flour

3½ cups (700g, 1½ lb) strawberries, hulled and quartered

7 cups (700g, 1½ lb) fresh blueberries

¾ cup (245g, 9oz) apricot jam

¼ cup (60ml, 2fl oz) Madeira wine

1⅔ cups (400ml, 13fl oz) thickened cream

½ cup (110g, 4oz) caster sugar

1 tsp vanilla extract

1 x 500g pack savoiardi sponge finger biscuits, cut into 3cm (1in) pieces

METHOD

1. To make the custard, place the milk, cream and vanilla in a medium saucepan over medium heat. Cook, stirring, for 12 minutes until almost boiling. Pour into a bowl and set aside to cool for at least 20 minutes.

2. Whisk egg yolks, sugar and arrowroot flour together in a medium saucepan until pale and creamy. Gradually whisk in the warm milk mixture, ensuring there are no lumps. Return to the stovetop and cook over medium heat for 12 minutes, stirring the whole time. Once the liquid coats the back of a spoon, it is ready. Chill the custard in the refrigerator for at least 3 hours to thicken before using in the trifle.

3. Set aside ¾ cup each of the strawberries and blueberries for the topping.

4. Gently heat the apricot jam in a small saucepan over medium heat until it has become a liquid. Let it cool for 15 minutes, then add to a large mixing bowl with the berries and wine and gently toss to coat the berries.

5. Whip the cream, sugar and vanilla together until stiff peaks form. Set aside in the refrigerator to chill.

6. To assemble the trifle, place a layer of biscuits on the bottom of a large glass trifle dish. Place one third of the fruit mixture over the top, then layer with one third of the custard. Repeat until you have a top layer of custard. Spread the whipped cream mixture over the top.

7. Refrigerate for at least 4 hours, preferably overnight, to let the sponge biscuits soak up the liquid.

8. Before serving, top with the reserved fruit.

CHOCOLATE LOVERS

DARK CHOCOLATE GANACHE AND MARZIPAN CAKE

INGREDIENTS

¾ cup (90g, 3oz) plus 1 tbsp plain flour

1½ cups (185g, 6oz) flaked almonds, chopped

Pinch of salt

140g (5oz) unsalted butter, room temperature, chopped

180g (6oz) almond paste, crumbled into small pieces

¾ cup (165g, 6oz) caster sugar

1 tsp vanilla extract

1 tsp almond extract

5 eggs, room temperature

¼ cup (60ml, 2fl oz) Cointreau

55g (2oz) semi-sweet dark cooking chocolate, grated

Ganache

¾ cup (185ml, 6fl oz) thickened cream

⅓ cup (70g, 2½ oz) caster sugar

300g (10oz) dark cooking chocolate (60-72%), chopped

½ tbsp vanilla extract

1 cup (125g, 4oz) pistachios, finely chopped

12 fresh raspberries

METHOD

1. Preheat the oven to 160°C (325°F, Gas Mark 3) and line a 23cm (9in) cake tin with greased baking paper.

2. Pulse together the flour, almonds and salt in a food processor until the almonds are ground to a very fine meal, then set aside.

3. Beat the butter, almond paste and sugar together until the mixture resembles fluffy whipped cream. Beat in the vanilla and almond extracts. Add the eggs one at a time, incorporating each completely before adding the next one, then mix the Cointreau through. Stir in the flour mixture until just mixed through. Fold in the grated chocolate then pour the mixture into the cake tin.

4. Bake for about 35 minutes or until a skewer inserted into the middle comes out clean. Let cool for 5 minutes in the tin before removing to a wire rack to cool completely.

5. To make the ganache, bring the cream and sugar to a boil in a small saucepan over medium heat. Pour the heated cream over the chocolate with the vanilla and let sit for 3 minutes before gently stirring to combine. Let the ganache cool and thicken slightly before using.

6. Coat the cake on the top and sides with the ganache and press the pistachios into the side of the cake. Decorate with the raspberries and sprinkle any leftover pistachios on the top. Chill for at least 1 hour to set the ganache.

Note: You can reserve ½ cup of the ganache and pipe 12 small fluted flourishes around the edge of the cake and press the raspberries into those to completely decorate the cake.

CHOCOLATE LOAF CAKE

INGREDIENTS

Cake

120g (4oz) dark cooking chocolate, roughly chopped

250g (9oz) unsalted butter

2 cups (300g, 10oz) brown sugar

2 large eggs, room temperature

1 tsp vanilla extract

1¼ cup (160g, 5oz) plain flour

1 tsp bicarbonate of soda

1 cup (260ml, 9fl oz) boiling water

Icing

⅓ cup (80ml, 3fl oz) thickened cream

175g (6oz) white cooking chocolate

METHOD

1. Preheat the oven to 190°C (375°F, Gas Mark 5) and grease a loaf tin.

2. Melt the chocolate in a heat-resistant bowl over a saucepan of gently simmering water. Then set aside to cool.

3. Cream the butter and sugar together until they resemble whipped cream. Beat in the eggs one at a time with the vanilla.

4. Add the melted, slightly cooled chocolate and roughly mix through.

5. Sift the flour and bicarb together, then add the flour and the water in thirds to the chocolate mix, combining both well after each addition until you have a smooth batter.

6. Pour into the loaf tin and bake for 20 minutes, then reduce the temperature to 160°C (325°F, Gas Mark 3) and bake for a further 25 minutes, until a skewer inserted into the middle comes out clean. Let it cool on a wire rack for at least 1 hour before icing.

7. To make the icing, heat the cream in a small saucepan over medium heat until almost simmering. Remove from heat and gently stir in the chocolate. Let sit for 5 minutes before using.

CHOCOLATE SAUCE

INGREDIENTS

1 cup (250ml, 8fl oz) water

½ cup (100g, 3oz) caster sugar

½ cup (160g, 5oz) agave syrup

¾ cup (75g, 3oz) cacao powder

55g (2oz) dark cooking chocolate, chopped

METHOD

1. Whisk together the water, sugar, agave and cacao in a medium saucepan over medium heat for 8 minutes until the sugar is dissolved and it just starts to boil.

2. Remove the pan from the heat and gently stir in the chopped chocolate until it's melted and combined.

3. Let it cool for at least 1 hour before serving.

    Note: Will keep in the fridge in a sealed container for up to 2 weeks.

SERVES 6 ★ PREP 30min (PLUS CHILLING) ★ COOK TIME 10min

CHOCOLATE CHERRY SLICE

INGREDIENTS

Chocolate layer

250g (9oz) unsalted butter, room temperature

1½ cups (350g, 12oz) caster sugar

2 large eggs, room temperature

100g (3½ oz) unsweetened cooking chocolate

1 tsp vanilla extract

½ cup (60g, 2oz) cocoa

1 tsp bicarbonate of soda

½ tsp salt

3 cups (380g, 12oz) plain flour

Cheesecake layer

90g (3oz) white cooking chocolate, roughly chopped

250g (9oz) cream cheese

100g (3½ oz) mascarpone

⅓ cup (60g, 2oz) icing sugar

1 large egg, room temperature

3 cups (420g, 15oz) pitted preserved sour cherries, drained, juice reserved

Cherry syrup

1½ tbsps caster sugar

METHOD

1. Preheat the oven to 170°C (340°F, Gas Mark 4) and line a 5cm (2in) deep, 18cm (7in) square cake tin with baking paper.

2. To make the base, beat the butter and sugar together until it resembles whipped cream. Add the eggs one at a time, completely mixing each one in before adding the next. Melt the chocolate in a heatproof bowl over a saucepan of simmering water. Remove from the heat and let cool for 10 minutes, then whisk it with the vanilla into the butter mixture. Sift the cocoa, bicarb and salt into the flour then fold it into the mixture a third at a time. Reserve just under one quarter of the batter and pour the rest into the baking tin. Bake for 20 minutes then remove and let cool to room temperature.

3. To make the cheesecake layer, melt the white chocolate in a heatproof bowl over a saucepan of simmering water. Remove from the heat and let cool for 10 minutes. Beat in the cream cheese, mascarpone and sugar until smooth. Beat in the egg until mixed thorugh thoroughly. Gently stir through 1 cup of the cherries. Pour the cheesecake mix on top of the base and press another ½ cup of cherries into the cheesecake mix.

4. Spread the reserved chocolate batter over the top. Use a knife to make a couple of swirls in the top to let the cheesecake show through. Bake for 30 minutes until set. Let cool for 1 hour then chill in the refrigerator for 3 hours.

5. To make the cherry syrup, place the sugar and 1 cup of the reserved cherry juice in a medium saucepan over medium-high heat and bring to a boil. Reduce to a simmer and let it cook for about 20 minutes until reduced and thickened. Let cool for 20 minutes and stir the rest of the cherries through.

6. Cut the slice into roughly 4cm (1½ in) squares and top with cherries and syrup.

CHOCOLATE CHERRY PARFAIT

INGREDIENTS

Mousse

100g (3½ oz) milk cooking chocolate

2 eggs, separated

⅔ cup (150ml, 5fl oz) thickened cream

Cherry syrup

1½ cups (285g, 10oz) maraschino cherries, roughly chopped

2 tbsps caster sugar

1 cup (250ml, 8fl oz) water

2½ cups (250g, 9oz) chocolate ripple biscuits, roughly crumbled

6 whole cherries with stem intact

6 chocolate swirl wafers

1 cup caramel cream (see recipe page 19), gently heated until warm

METHOD

1. To make the mousse, melt chocolate in a heat-resistant bowl over a saucepan of gently simmering water. Remove from the heat and gently whisk in the egg yolks. Set aside to cool for at least 30 minutes.

2. In a large bowl, whip cream until soft peaks form. Use a slotted spoon to gently fold cream through the chocolate mixture.

2. Beat the egg whites until stiff peaks form. Gently fold the egg whites into the chocolate mixture until combined. Chill for at least 4 hours before using.

3. Place 2 tablespoons of cherries, the sugar and water in a medium saucepan over medium heat and bring to a boil and then reduce to a simmer for 20 minutes until thickened. Stir in the rest of the cherries, remove from heat and let cool.

4. To assemble, place a tablespoon of mousse in the bottom of each dessert glass. Top with ¼ cup crumbled biscuits, then a large spoonful of the cherries. Repeat. Top each with two whole cherries, a wafer and a large spoonful of warm caramel sauce.

SERVES 10 ★ PREP 20MIN (PLUS CHILLING) ★ COOK TIME 40MIN

CHOCOLATE RASPBERRY TART

INGREDIENTS

Crust

2 cups (200g, 7oz) Granita biscuits, loosely crumbled

½ cup (80g, 3oz) light brown sugar

Salt

½ cup (125g, 4oz) butter, melted

Filling

350g (12oz) dark cooking chocolate, roughly chopped

1¾ cups (440ml, 15fl oz) thickened cream

2 tbsps caster sugar

½ tsp vanilla extract

1½ cups (185g, 6oz) fresh raspberries

METHOD

1. Preheat the oven to 180°C (350°F, Gas Mark 4) and lightly grease a 25cm (10in) round fluted tart tin with a removable bottom.

2. Process the biscuits, sugar and pinch of salt in a food processor with until it forms a fine meal. Add the melted butter and pulse to combine. Press firmly into the bottom and up the sides of the tin.

3. Line with foil and fill with baking beads. Blind bake for 8 minutes. Place on a wire rack to cool for at least 30 minutes before filling.

4. Combine the chocolate and another pinch of salt in a large mixing bowl. Heat 1¼ cups of cream in a small saucepan until almost simmering. Pour the cream over the chocolate and gently stir to combine. (The less you stir, the glossier the chocolate mix will be.)

5. Pour the chocolate mix into the tart case and refrigerate until set, for at least 2 hours.

6. When tart is set, heat the remaining cream with the sugar and vanilla until almost simmering. Drizzle the warm cream over the chocolate filling. Use a toothpick to create a marbling effect in the chocolate.

6. Top with the raspberries and serve.

CHOCOLATE ROULADE

INGREDIENTS

200g (7oz) dark cooking chocolate, roughly chopped

¼ cup (30g, 1oz) Dutch cocoa powder

4 eggs, room temperature

½ cup (110g, 4oz) caster sugar

1 cup (275ml, 9fl oz)

raspberries, halved

METHOD

1. Preheat the oven to 180°C (350°F, Gas Mark 4) and a 25 x 30cm (10 x 12in) Swiss roll pan with baking paper.

2. Melt the chocolate in a large heatproof bowl over a pot of simmering water. Stir in 1 tablespoon of the cocoa. P move from heat.

3. Separate the eggs and beat the yolks together with the sugar until pale and creamy. Stir the egg mixture into the chocolate mixture.

4. Beat the egg whites until stiff peaks form. Use a slotted spoon to fold the egg whites into the chocolate mixture until mixed through.

5. Spread the chocolate mixture into the pan and bake for 10 minutes.

6. Place a large sheet of baking paper on a wire rack and sprinkle the baking paper with half of the remaining cocoa powder.

7. Carefully turn the cake out on top of the prepared baking paper, then let the cake cool for at least 1 hour before moving on to the next step.

8. Whip the cream until it begins to form stiff peaks. Spread the cream over the top of the cake and dot with raspberries. Use the paper to roll up the cake to form the roulade. Sprinkle with the remaining cocoa powder and serve.

SALTED CARAMEL AND CHOCOLATE MERINGUES

INGREDIENTS

Meringues

4 large egg whites, room temperature

1 tsp white vinegar

1 cup (220g, 8oz) caster sugar

100g (3½ oz) dark cooking chocolate

Chocolate sauce

½ cup (125ml, 4fl oz) water

¼ cup (50g, 2oz) caster sugar

¼ cup (80g, 3oz) agave syrup

⅓ cup (40g) cacao powder

30g (1oz) dark cooking chocolate, chopped

Caramel sauce

1 cup (155g, 5oz) light brown sugar

90g (3oz) unsalted butter, room temperature, roughly chopped

½ cup (125ml, 4fl oz) thickened cream, room temperature

½ tbsp sea salt

METHOD

1. To make the meringues, preheat oven to 150°C (300°F, Gas Mark 2) and line two large flat baking trays with baking paper that has four 8cm (3in) circles drawn on each piece.

2. Beat egg whites until stiff peaks form. Add the vinegar and then caster sugar, one third at a time, until mixture is thick and glossy.

3. Melt the chocolate in a small heatproof bowl over a saucepan of simmering water.

4. Divide the meringue mix evenly between trays, placing round dollops in the centre of each circle. Flatten the tops slightly and spread out to fit the circles. Drizzle 1 teaspoon of melted chocolate over the meringues, one at a time. Use a toothpick to swirl the chocolate around in each meringue.

5. Reduce oven temperature to 120°C (250°F, Gas Mark 1) and place the trays in the oven. Bake meringues for 30 minutes, or until they are crisp on the outside when touched. Turn off the oven, leaving it closed, and let the meringues cool for 2 hours before removing.

6. To make the chocolate sauce, whisk together the water, sugar, agave and cacao in a small saucepan over medium heat for 6 minutes until sugar is dissolved. Remove from the heat and gently stir in the chopped chocolate until it's melted..

7. To make the caramel sauce, heat the sugar in a saucepan over medium-high heat until it starts to melt. Stir briskly until all melted. Continue to cook until it begins to turn golden, then whisk in the butter gradually. (Remove from the heat briefly if it looks like turning darker-than-golden. Do not let it burn!) Remove the pot from the heat and gradually add the cream. Stir until thickened and smooth. Add the salt and stir through.

8. To serve, drizzle with the chocolate and caramel sauces.

WHITE STRAWBERRIES

INGREDIENTS

2½ cups (500g, 1lb 2oz) firm ripe strawberries

600g (1lb 5oz) white cooking chocolate

¼ cup (60ml, 2fl oz) thickened cream

2 drops yellow food colouring

METHOD

1. Wash the strawberries then pat completely dry with a paper towel.

2. Melt two-thirds of the chocolate in a heat-resistant bowl over a saucepan of gently simmering water.

3. Line a large flat tray with baking paper.

4. Dip each strawberry in the melted chocolate and place on the baking tray.

5. Once the strawberries are finished, melt the rest of the chocolate and then stir through the cream and the food colouring.

6. Place the coloured chocolate into a piping bag and pipe a few thin lines over each strawberry. Let them sit for about 1 hour to let the chocolate harden.

CHOCOLATE TRUFFLES

INGREDIENTS

Truffles

1¼ cups (310ml, 10fl oz) thickened cream

255g (9oz) dark cooking chocolate (70% cocoa), roughly chopped

Chocolate coating

130g (4oz) dark cooking chocolate (70% cocoa), finely chopped

¼ cup (30g, 1oz) cacao powder

¼ cup (20g, ¾ oz) desiccated coconut

80g (3oz) white cooking chocolate

METHOD

1. Heat the cream to simmer in a saucepan over medium-high heat. Take off the heat and let cool for 10 minutes.

2. Melt 190g of the chocolate in a heat-resistant bowl over a saucepan of simmering water. Remove from the heat then stir in the rest of the chocolate and cream until smooth. Chill the mixture in the refrigerator for 2 hours until it has firmed up.

3. Line two large flat trays with baking paper. Using hands, roll 2 tablespoons of the mixture into balls and place on prepared trays. Repeat with the rest of the mix. Chill until firm for 1 hour.

4. To make dark-chocolate-coated truffles, first heat the chocolate in a heat-resistant bowl over a saucepan of simmering water until just starting to melt. Remove from heat and place about 1 teaspoon of the melted chocolate in your palm. Roll the chilled truffle in your hand to coat it with the chocolate, then roll in the cacao or desiccated coconut and place on the tray.

5. To make white-chocolate-coated truffles, repeat step 4 with the white chocolate. Let the truffles chill for 1 hour before serving.

SERVES 6 ★ PREP 40MIN (PLUS COOLING) ★ COOK TIME 1HR 30MIN

CHOCOLATE CHERRY PAVLOVA LAYER CAKE

INGREDIENTS

Meringues

5 medium egg whites, at room temperature

¼ tsp salt

3 tsps arrowroot flour

1½ tsps white wine vinegar

¾ tsp vanilla extract

1½ cups (330g, 12oz) caster sugar

200g (7oz) dark cooking chocolate

Filling

4 cups (900g, 2lb) fresh cherries, 2 cups of which halved and pitted

⅓ cup (70g, 2½ oz) plus 1 tbsp caster sugar

1 tsp arrowroot flour

⅓ cup (80ml, 3fl oz) water

2½ cups (600ml, 21fl oz) thickened cream

½ tsp vanilla extract

¼ cup (40g, 1½ oz) dark chocolate, grated

METHOD

1. To make the meringues, preheat the oven to 200°C (400°F, Gas Mark 6) and line three baking trays with baking paper. Draw a 20cm (8in) circle on each sheet of paper.

2. Beat the egg whites and salt together in a mixing bowl until stiff peaks form. Add the arrowroot flour, vinegar, vanilla and sugar, a third at a time, mixing until dissolved after each addition, until the mixture is thick with firm, shiny peaks.

3. Divide the meringue between the three sheets and spread out to just inside the circles.

4. Melt the chocolate in a heat-resistant bowl over a saucepan of gently simmering water. Drizzle small amounts of the chocolate over the three meringues and use a butter knife to swirl it around in the meringues to make marbled patterns.

5. Turn the oven down to 180°C (350°F, Gas Mark 4) and bake the meringues for 1½ hours. Turn off the oven and let them cool in the oven for at least 2 hours before opening the door.

6. For the filling, place the cherry halves, ⅓ cup of sugar, arrowroot flour and water in a medium saucepan and cook over medium-high heat until the liquid is nearly simmering. Remove the cherries from the heat and let cool for 30 minutes.

7. Whip together the cream, 1 tablespoon of sugar and vanilla until soft peaks form.

8. To assemble, spread one-third of the cream over a meringue layer, then drizzle over one-third of the cherries in syrup. Place another meringue on top and again spread over one-third of the cream and one-third of the cherries in syrup. Place the last meringue over the top and spread over the remaining cream. Drizzle the rest of the cherries and syrup over the top, sprinkle with shaved chocolate and top with the whole cherries. Serve.

CHOCOLATE ORANGE MOUSSE

INGREDIENTS

8 medium eggs, separated, room temperature

½ cup (100g, 3½ oz) caster sugar

1 tbsp orange juice

2 tbsps cacao powder

1¼ cups (300ml, 10fl oz) thickened cream

½ cup (20g, ¾ oz) orange zest strands

METHOD

1. Beat together the egg yolks with the sugar until they are pale, light and more than doubled in size. Fold through the orange juice and cacao powder.

2. Whip the cream until soft peaks form, use a slotted spoon to fold in the chocolate mixture until thoroughly combined.

3. Beat the egg whites until stiff peaks start to form.

4. Gently fold the egg whites into the chocolate cream mixture.

5. Divide the mousse between four serving glasses or bowls. Cover and chill in the refrigerator for at least 4 hours, preferably overnight.

6. Serve decorated with strands of orange zest.

WHITE CHOCOLATE PUDDING

INGREDIENTS

160g (6oz) unsalted butter

300g (10oz) white cooking chocolate, roughly chopped

¾ cup (150g, 5oz) caster sugar

7 large eggs, room temperature

1 tsp vanilla extract

1¼ cups (160g, 5oz) plain flour

Pinch of salt

180g (6oz) cherries, pitted

3 tbsps icing sugar

¼ cup (60ml, 2fl oz) water

METHOD

1. Preheat the oven to 180°C (350°F, Gas Mark 4) and line eight ramekins with soft unsalted butter and lightly coat the insides with flour.

2. Melt the butter and white chocolate in a heatproof bowl over a saucepan of simmering water. Once melted, remove from heat.

3. Beat the sugar and eggs together until they are light and creamy. Then stir in the vanilla. Fold the chocolate into the egg mixture until thoroughly combined. Then fold in the flour and salt, ensuring it's mixed through completely.

4. Pour the mix into the ramekins until they're about three-quarters full. Bake for 12 minutes then remove from the oven.

5. Stir the cherries in a medium saucepan with the icing sugar and water over medium heat for 10 minutes until they start to soften and lose some juice. Remove from the heat and set aside.

6. Carefully invert the fondants onto serving plates and serve with cherries in syrup on top. Serve immediately while the chocolate is still melted and gooey on the inside.

CHOCOLATE AND RASPBERRY ICE-CREAM COOKIES

INGREDIENTS

Ice cream

1½ cups (185g, 6oz) frozen raspberries (or fresh)

2½ cups (600ml, 21fl oz) thickened cream

1 cup (250ml, 8fl oz) buttermilk

¾ cup (165g, 6oz) caster sugar

1 tsp vanilla extract

Biscuits

115g (4oz) unsalted butter, room temperature

½ cup (80g, 3oz) lightly packed brown sugar

½ cup (110g, 4oz) caster sugar

1 large egg, room temperature

½ tsp vanilla extract

1 cup (125g, 4oz) plain flour

½ cup (60g, 2oz) cacao powder

½ tsp bicarbonate of soda

Pinch of salt

METHOD

1. To make the ice cream, push the defrosted raspberries through a fine metal sieve into a bowl to remove the seeds and any solids.

2. Add the raspberry puree to a blender with the rest of the ice cream ingredients and blend.

3. Add to an ice-cream maker and mix for 30 minutes or until thickened. Remove to an ice-cream container and freeze for at least 4 hours, preferably overnight, before using.

4. To make the cookies, preheat the oven to 180°C (350°F, Gas Mark 4) and line a large flat baking tray with baking paper.

5. Beat together the butter and sugars until the mixture resembles whipped cream. Mix in the egg and vanilla and continue mixing until combined.

6. In a separate bowl, whisk together the flour, cacao powder, bicarb and salt. Add the flour mixture into the butter mixture one third at a time, ensuring each batch is completely incorporated. The dough with be thick and very sticky.

7. Portion out 24 dollops of dough onto the tray and slightly flatten the tops. Bake them for 8 minutes until the tops are almost set. Allow them to cool on the tray for 12 minutes, then let them cool completely on a wire rack.

8. To assemble, place a flattened scoop of ice cream between the flat sides of two biscuits and serve.

CHOCOLATE RUM BABA

INGREDIENTS

7g (¼ oz) yeast

3 tsps water, lukewarm

½ cup (80g, 3oz) raisins

¾ cup (200ml, 7fl oz) rum

2 cups (250g, 8oz) bread flour

Pinch of salt

1 tbsp caster sugar

125g (4oz) unsalted butter, room temperature

4 eggs, room temperature

Syrup

6 cups (1.5L, 50fl oz) water

4½ cups (1kg, 2lb) caster sugar

1 portion chocolate sauce (see recipe page 16)

METHOD

1. Dissolve the yeast in the warm water in a small bowl. In a separate bowl, soak the raisins in the rum. Sift together the flour, salt and sugar into a large mixing bowl and make a well in the middle. Add the yeast to flour and then mix in the butter then the eggs, one at a time, until a thick dough forms.

2. Drain the raisins, reserving the rum, and add the raisins and work them into the dough.

3. Grease the insides of 10 dariold moulds with melted butter and divide the mixture between them. Leave them in a warm place, covered with a damp tea towel, until the dough has risen to fill the moulds.

4. To make the syrup, gently heat the water and sugar together in a medium saucepan over medium heat for 10 minutes or until the sugar is dissolved. Remove from the heat and set aside.

5. Preheat the oven to 200°C (400°F, Gas Mark 6) and bake the babas for 20 minutes. Turn them out onto a wire rack resting over a dish.

6. First pour the reserved rum over the babas, ensuring it's all soaked up. Then pour over the syrup, collecting the excess in the dish. Spoon the syrup over them several times to ensure they're soaked through.

7. Dip the tops of the babas in the chocolate sauce and serve.

BLISS BALLS

INGREDIENTS

2 x 250g (9oz) packets Marie biscuits

2 x 400g (14oz) cans sweetened condensed milk

½ tbsp cacao powder

3 cups (270g, 9oz) desiccated coconut

METHOD

1. Place the biscuits in a blender and pulse until they resemble breadcrumbs.

2. Add the biscuit crumbs, condensed milk and cacao into a large mixing bowl. Mix together until thoroughly combined.

3. Roll tablespoons of the mixture into bite-size balls.Place the coconut in a bowl and roll the balls in it until they're coated in coconut.

   Note: These will keep in the refrigerator in an airtight container for up to 10 days.

CHOCOLATE CHEESECAKE BROWNIES

INGREDIENTS

Chocolate layer

90g (3oz) unsalted butter, room temperature

120g (4oz) milk cooking chocolate

2/3 cup (100g, 3oz) light brown sugar

2 large eggs, room temperature

½ cup (60g, 2oz) plain flour

1 tbsp Dutch cocoa powder

Pinch of salt

1 tsp vanilla extract

Cheesecake

225g (8oz) cream cheese, room temperature, cut into cubes

1 large egg yolk, room temperature

5 tbsps caster sugar

½ tsp lemon zest

1 cup (100g, 3½ oz) fresh or frozen blueberries

2 tbsps icing sugar

METHOD

1. Preheat the oven to 180°C (350°F, Gas Mark 4) and line a 23cm (9in) square slice tin with greased baking paper.

2. In a saucepan, melt the butter and chocolate over low heat, stirring until smooth. Whisk in the sugar, then remove from the heat.

3. Whisk in the eggs, one at a time, ensuring each is thoroughly mixed through.

4. In a large mixing bowl, sift together the flour, cocoa and salt. Fold in the chocolate mix with the vanilla. Spread two-thirds of the mixture in the bottom of the slice tin.

5. In a separate bowl, whisk together the cream cheese, egg yolk, sugar and lemon zest.

6. Carefully dollop the cream cheese over the base and then use a flat spatula to swirl it over the chocolate batter in a layer.

7. Pour the rest of the chocolate mix over the top, then press the blueberries deep into the top layer.

8. Bake for 40 minutes or until cooked through. Let cool for 5 minutes, then remove to a wire rack to cool for at least another 30 minutes.

9. Dust the top with icing sugar, then cut the slice into squares and serve.

WHITE CHOCOLATE SWIRL

INGREDIENTS

1½ cups (375ml, 13fl oz) thickened cream

½ cup (80g, 3oz) white cooking chocolate

3 cups (375g, 13oz) fresh raspberries

2 tbsps caster sugar

¼ cup (60ml, 2fl oz) sparkling wine (optional)

½ cup (125ml, 4fl oz) Greek yoghurt

1 tsp vanilla extract

½ cup (80g, 3oz) milk chocolate, grated, reserve 2 tbsps for garnish

METHOD

1. Preheat the oven to 180°C (350°F, Gas Mark 4) and line a small baking tray with baking paper.

2. Heat ½ cup of cream in a small saucepan until it's almost simmering then remove from heat and stir in the white chocolate until it's melted. Set aside.

3. Using a blender, pulse the raspberries a few times. Remove them to a mixing bowl and stir in the sugar and sparkling wine.

4. Whip the rest of the cream until peaks form. Use a slotted spoon to fold in the yoghurt, vanilla, grated choclate and white chocolate cream.

5. Layer the cream and raspberry mixtures into serving glasses, placing a dollop of cream first, then a layer of raspberry then top with the cream.

6. Garnish with some grated chocolate.

SERVES 6 ★ PREP 40MIN (PLUS CHILLING) ★ COOK TIME 20MIN

WHITE CHOC-MINT MOUSSE

INGREDIENTS

2 cups (500ml, 1pt) thickened cream

350g (12oz) white cooking chocolate, roughly chopped

¼ tsp peppermint extract

6 sprigs of mint, to garnish

METHOD

1. Heat 1/4 of the cream in a small heavy-based saucepan over medium heat until almost simmering. Turn the heat down to low and stir in the chocolate until just melted. Remove from heat and stir in the peppermint essence. Let cool for 20 minutes.

2. Whip the rest of the cream until stiff peaks form.

3. Gently fold the chocolate mixture into the whipped cream until mixed through.

4. Divide the mixture between 6 serving glasses and chill in the refrigerator for 4 hours, preferably overnight.

5. Serve garnished with mint sprigs.

SERVES 10 ★ **PREP 40**MIN (PLUS CHILLING) ★ **COOK TIME 1**HR **35**MIN

WHITE CHOCOLATE CREAM CHEESECAKE

INGREDIENTS

115g (4oz) unsalted butter, room temperature

¾ cup (165g, 6oz) caster sugar

1 tsp vanilla extract

1 cup (125g, 4oz) plain flour

370g (13oz) white cooking chocolate, roughly chopped

1kg (2lb) cream cheese, room temperature, cubed

4 large eggs, room temperature

½ cup (100g, 3½ oz) fresh strawberries, halved

METHOD

1. Preheat the oven to 190°C (375°F, Gas Mark 5) and line the bottom of a 23cm (9in) springform cake tin.

2. To make the base, beat together the butter, ¼ cup of sugar and half the vanilla with a mixer until it resembles whipped cream, then mix the flour through.

3. Press the mixture into the bottom of the cake tin. Prick lightly all over with a fork. Bake for 25 minutes or until the edge is lightly browned.

4. To make the filling, melt the chocolate in a heatproof bowl over a pot of simmering water, then remove from heat. Spread a large dessertspoonful over a sheet of baking paper in a thin layer and leave to cool.

5. Beat the cream cheese with the rest of the sugar and vanilla in large bowl with a mixer until well blended. Stir in the melted chocolate and mix through thoroughly. Add the eggs, one at a time, ensuring each is just mixed through before adding the next. Pour the mix over the base.

6. Bake for 1 hour or until the centre is almost set. Run a knife around the edge of the tin to loosen the cake but let it cool before releasing the springform casing.

7. Refrigerate for at least 5 hours before serving. Use a knife to shave pieces from the hardened smear of chocolate on the baking paper and use to decorate the cake along with fresh strawberries. Serve.

CHOCOLATE SLICE

INGREDIENTS

½ cup (60g, 2oz) plain flour

½ cup (60g, 2oz) almond meal

½ cup (60g, 2oz) cacao powder

1½ tsps bicarbonate of soda

½ tsp salt

¼ tsp ground cardamom

120g (4oz) butter, room temperature

1 cup (220g, 8oz) caster sugar

1 cup (155g, 5oz) brown sugar

2 large eggs, room temperature

1 tsp vanilla extract

½ cup (125ml, 4fl oz) buttermilk

1 cup (250ml, 8fl oz) lukewarm water

2 cups (250g, 8oz) whole almonds

¼ cup (30g, 1oz) almonds, roughly chopped

METHOD

1. Preheat the oven to 160°C (325°F, Gas Mark 3) and line a large slice tin with baking paper.

2. Sift the flour, almond meal, cacao, bicarb, salt and cardamom together.

3. Beat the butter and sugars together until the mixture resembles whipped cream, then beat in the eggs one at a time with the vanilla.

4. Stir the flour, buttermilk and water in, a third at a time, ensuring everything is just mixed together after each addition.

5. Pour into the slice tin and bake for 30 minutes, or until a skewer inserted into the middle of the slice comes out clean.

6. Remove from the oven, decorate with almonds and cut into squares to serve.

CHOCOLATE PRALINES

INGREDIENTS

2½ cups (310g, 10oz) hazelnuts

250g (9oz) unsweetened dark cooking chocolate, roughly chopped.

1 tbsp caster sugar

½ tsp salt

METHOD

1. Preheat the oven to 200°C (400°F, Gas Mark 6) and line a large flat baking tray with baking paper. Roast the hazelnuts in the oven for 6 minutes until they start to brown.

2. Remove them from the oven and tip out in a single layer onto a tea towel. Line the tray again with a clean sheet of baking paper for later. Cover the hazelnuts with a second tea towel and rub them to get the skins off. Use your hands to remove any remaining pieces of skin, but you can leave a small amount on them.

3. Melt the chocolate and sugar in a large heat-resistant bowl over a saucepan of gently simmering water. Remove from the heat, stir in the salt and gently stir through. (The less you stir, the glossier the chocolate will be.)

4. Tip the hazelnuts into the chocolate mixture and gently stir to coat them in the chocolate. Use two forks to remove the nuts to the baking tray and refrigerate them for 30 minutes until the chocolate has hardened.

CHOCOLATE DOUGHNUTS

INGREDIENTS

100g (3½ oz) dark cooking chocolate

40g (1½ oz) unsalted butter, room temperature

½ cup (50g, 2oz) Dutch cocoa powder

1 cup (150g, 5oz) light brown sugar

1 tbsp vanilla extract

2 large eggs, room temperature, lightly beaten

2 cups (250g, 8oz) plain flour

1 tsp bicarbonate of soda

1 tsp baking powder

¾ cup (185ml, 6fl oz) milk

1 portion chocolate sauce (see recipe page 16)

METHOD

1. Preheat the oven to 180°C (350°F, Gas Mark 4) and grease two 6-hole large muffin tins (or you can use the same one twice over, it won't affect the doughnuts).

2. Melt the chocolate and butter together in a heatproof bowl over a saucepan of simmering water. Stir in the cocoa, sugar and vanilla and then remove from the heat.

3. Beat in the eggs, one at a time, ensuring each is thoroughly mixed through before adding the next.

4. Mix the flour, bicarb and baking powder together, then add to the chocolate mixture with the milk in thirds, ensuring everything is just mixed before the next addition.

5. Tear off six or twelve 8 x 8cm (3 x 3in) pieces of greaseproof paper, lightly wet them and then scrunch each into a small ball.

6. Place the paper balls in the centre of each hole in the tins.

7. Pour the chocolate doughnut mixture around each paper ball, being careful not to cover them. Bake the doughnuts for 12 minutes.

8. Let them cool in the tin for about 10 minutes then pull out the paper balls.

9. Heat the chocolate sauce over medium heat for 5 minutes until just warm. Dip the tops of the doughnuts in the sauce and serve.

CHOC MERINGUE CUPCAKES

INGREDIENTS

Cupcakes

190g (7oz) unsweetened dark cooking chocolate, chopped

¾ cup (180ml, 6fl oz) unsalted butter, melted, cooled

⅔ cup (70g, 2½ oz) cacao powder

¾ cup (165g, 6oz) caster sugar

¾ cup (120g, 4oz) light brown sugar

¼ cup (50ml, 2fl oz) apple cider vinegar

2 tsps vanilla extract

3 eggs

1½ cups (185g, 6oz) plain flour

½ tsp salt

1 tsp bicarbonate of soda

1½ cups (375ml, 13fl oz) milk

Meringue

4 large egg whites

½ tsp cream of tartar

1 cup (220g, 8oz) sugar

Chocolate magic topping

250g (9oz) milk cooking chocolate, finely chopped

200g (7oz) coconut oil

⅓ cup (125g, 4oz) agave syrup

METHOD

1. Preheat the oven to 180°C (350°F, Gas Mark 4) and line two 12-hole cupcake tins. Melt chocolate and butter in a heatproof bowl over a saucepan of simmering water. Stir in cacao, sugars, vinegar and vanilla and then remove from heat. Beat in eggs, one at a time. Mix flour, salt and bicarb together, then add to the chocolate mixture with the milk in thirds. Pour mixture into the cupcake liners. Bake for 18 minutes. Remove to a wire rack to cool.

2. Increase oven to 230°C (450°F, Gas Mark 8). Beat egg whites and cream of tartar until stiff peaks form. Pour in the sugar in thirds, whisking until stiff and glossy. Transfer meringue to a Ziploc bag with an opening in one corner. Pipe onto each cupcake in an upward spiral. Bake for 4 minutes until lightly browned. Remove to a rack to cool completely.

3. Melt the topping ingredients together in a heatproof bowl over a pot of simmering water. Dip the meringues in the sauce and place the cupcakes in the fridge for at least 30 minutes to harden.

CHOC COCONUT PANNA COTTA

INGREDIENTS

1 x 400g (14 oz) can coconut milk

7g (¼ oz) gelatine powder

2 tbsps caster sugar

120g (4oz) white cooking chocolate

1 tsp vanilla extract

¼ cup (20g, ¾ oz) desiccated coconut

METHOD

1. Pour the coconut milk into a medium saucepan and whisk until smooth. Sprinkle the gelatine over the top and let it sit for a couple of minutes.

2. Turn the heat on to medium and add the sugar and chocolate. Dissolve the gelatine, sugar, and chocolate in the liquid, stirring constantly until the mixture is almost simmering. Remove from the heat.

3. Strain the liquid through a wire sieve. Then pour into six ramekins and chill in the refrigerator for at least 4 hours, preferably overnight.

4. Serve sprinkled with desiccated coconut.

THREE-LAYER CHOCOLATE MOUSSE CAKE

INGREDIENTS

Crust

1 x packet chocolate ripple biscuits, crushed

80g (3oz) butter, melted

Dark chocolate mousse

150g (5oz) dark chocolate

½ cup (125ml, 4fl oz) plus ⅔ cup (160ml, 5fl oz) thickened cream

1 level tsp gelatine powder

1 tbsp cold water

Milk chocolate mousse

150g (5 oz) milk chocolate

½ cup (125ml, 4fl oz) plus ⅔ cup (160ml, 5fl oz) thickened cream

1 level tsp gelatine powder

1 tbsp cold water

White chocolate mousse

150g (5 oz) white chocolate

½ cup (125ml, 4fl oz) plus ⅔ cup (160ml, 5fl oz) thickened cream

1 level tsp gelatine powder

1 tbsp cold water

Topping

50g (2oz) each dark , milk and white chocolate

METHOD

1. To make the crust, mix together the crushed biscuits and butter until combined, then press into the bottom of a high 20cm (8in) springform cake tin. Cool in the refrigerator while making the first batch of mousse.

2. To prepare the dark chocolate mousse, heat the dark chocolate and ½ cup cream in a heatproof bowl over a simmering pot of water. Gently stir until the chocolate is melted.

3. Dissolve the gelatine in the water, then heat in the microwave for 10 seconds. Stir then whisk into the chocolate.

4. Whip the rest of the cream until stiff peaks form. Use a slotted spoon to fold the chocolate into the whipped cream. Spread the mousse evenly over the base, then refrigerate for at least 1 hour before repeating steps 2 to 4 for the next two mousses.

5. Let the entire cake set in the refrigerator for at least 4 hours, preferably overnight.

6. To make the decorations, melt the chocolates separately in heatproof bowls over a simmering pot of water.

7. Use a spatula to spread wide streaks of melted chocolate over some baking paper. Once cooled, carefully peel off the leaves of chocolate, break up as desired and decorate the top of the cake with them.

BRANDY SNAPS WITH WHITE CHOCOLATE CREAM

INGREDIENTS

100g (3½ oz) unsalted butter, cut into cubes

½ cup (70g, 3oz) light brown sugar

⅓ cup (115g, 4oz) golden syrup

⅓ cup (50g, 1½ oz) plain flour

2 tbsps brandy

1 tsp ground ginger

½ tsp allspice

1¼ cups (300ml, 10fl oz) thickened cream

1 tbsp icing sugar

¼ tsp ground cinnamon

¼ tsp vanilla extract

Strips of orange zest, to garnish

METHOD

1. Preheat the oven to 150°C (300°F, Gas Mark 2) and line two baking trays with lightly greased baking paper.

2. Melt butter in a medium saucepan over low heat. Stir in the brown sugar and golden syrup until the sugar is dissolved. Then stir in the flour, brandy, ginger and allspice until combined. Remove from heat and allow to cool for at least 15 minutes.

3. Drop four teaspoons of the mix on to each tray, leaving space around each. Bake for 8 minutes or until the biscuits have spread to about 10cm (4in) in diameter and are bubbling.

4. Allow to cool for 10 seconds only, then as quickly as possible, use a flat knife to lift each one and wrap loosely around the handle of a wooden spoon. Allow to cool for 1 minute, then gently slide off the handle and repeat with the remaining snaps..

5. Whip the cream with the sugar, cinnamon and vanilla until stiff. Pipe the cream into each brandy snap and garnish with zest.

WHITE CHOCOLATE AND RASPBERRY BROWNIES

INGREDIENTS

150g (5oz) white cooking chocolate, roughly chopped

90g (3oz) unsalted butter, room temperature, cubed

⅔ cup (140g, 5oz) caster sugar

2 large eggs, room temperature

½ tsp vanilla extract

1¼ cups (140g, 5oz) plain flour

¼ tsp baking powder

¼ tsp ground cardamom

Pinch of salt

1 cup (125g, 4oz) fresh or frozen raspberries, chopped in half

METHOD

1. Preheat the oven to 180°C (350°F, Gas Mark 4) and line a 20cm (8in) square slice tin with greased baking paper.

2. Melt the chocolate and butter together in a heatproof bowl over a pot of simmering water, then remove from heat. Gently stir through the sugar. Let sit for 5 minutes to cool slightly.

3. Whisk in the eggs, one at a time, with the vanilla. Mix through the flour, baking powder, cardamom and salt. Then gently stir through half the raspberries. Pour the mixture into the slice tin.

4. Push the remaining raspberries into the top of the mix. Bake for 30 minutes or until just cooked.

5. Cool on a wire rack then cut into small pieces as desired.

CHOCOLATE BROWNIES WITH SALTED CARAMEL SAUCE

INGREDIENTS

Brownies

250g (9oz) butter, roughly chopped

½ cup (80g, 3oz) dark cooking chocolate, roughly chopped

½ cup (60g, 2oz) Dutch cocoa

1½ cups (330g, 12oz) caster sugar

4 medium eggs, room temperature

1 tsp vanilla essence

1 cup (125g, 4oz) plain flour

1 tsp baking powder

Sauce

2 cups (310g, 10oz) light brown sugar

175g (6oz) unsalted butter, room temperature, roughly chopped

1 cup (250ml, 8fl oz) thickened cream, room temperature

1 tbsp sea salt

¼ cup (30g, 1oz) walnuts, chopped, to garnish

METHOD

1. Preheat the oven to 180°C (350°F, Gas Mark 4) and line an 18 x 28cm (7 x 11in) slice tin with greased baking paper.

2. Melt butter and chocolate together in a large saucepan over medium heat for 8 minutes or until the chocolate is just melted. Stir in the cocoa then remove from heat and stir in the sugar.

3. Add the eggs and vanilla essence and mix through. Then sift in the flour and baking powder and stir through thoroughly.

4. Spoon into the slice tin and bake for 25 minutes until the top is cooked; you still want the inside gooey if possible.

5. While the brownies are cooking, heat the brown sugar in a heavy medium saucepan over medium-high heat until it just starts to melt. Immediately begin stirring it briskly until all melted. Let it cook until it begins to turn golden. As soon as it does, whisk in the butter gradually. Remove from the heat briefly if it looks like turning a darker-than-golden colour. Do not let it burn!

6. Once all the butter is stirred in, remove the pot from the heat and gradually add the cream. Stir until thickened and smooth. Add the salt and stir through.

7. Serve the hot brownies with a scoop of ice cream and hot salted caramel sauce drizzled over and garnished with chopped walnuts.

FRUITYFA-VOURITES

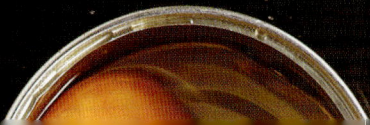

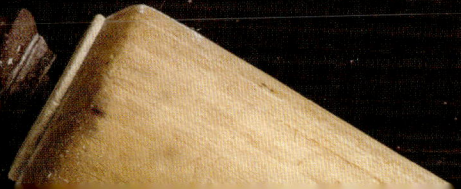

RASPBERRY CREAM PIE

INGREDIENTS

Base

115g (4oz) unsalted butter, room temperature

¾ cup (165g, 6oz) caster sugar

½ tsp vanilla extract

1 cup (125g, 4oz) plain flour

Topping

1 tbsp arrowroot flour

¼ cup (55g, 2oz) caster sugar

2 cups (250g, 8oz) fresh raspberries

1½ tsps water

1½ tsps fresh lemon juice

1 tbsp unsalted butter

½ tsp vanilla extract

Pinch of salt

Filling

3 cups (750ml, 24fl oz) thickened cream

230g (8oz) cream cheese, softened

¼ cup (55g, 2oz) caster sugar

½ tsp vanilla essence

Pinch of salt

½ cup (125ml, 4fl oz) sour cream

1 tbsp icing sugar

METHOD

1. To make the base, preheat the oven to 190°C (375°F, Gas Mark 5) and line the bottom of a 23cm (9in) springform cake tin.

2. Beat together the butter, sugar and vanilla with a mixer until it resembles whipped cream then mix the flour through.

3. Press the mixture into the bottom of the cake tin. Prick lightly all over with a fork. Bake for 25 minutes or until the edge is very lightly browned. Let cool for at least 1 hour.

4. To make the topping, place the arrowroot and sugar into a medium-sized saucepan over medium heat and stir to mix.

5. Add 1 heaped cup of raspberries. Gently stir in the water and lemon juice. Bring the mixture to a boil, stirring all the while. Reduce to a simmer and cook for 5 minutes or until the berries have broken down. Then remove from heat.

6. Stir in the butter, vanilla and salt until the butter is all melted and mixed through. Remove from the heat and let cool completely for at least 2 hours.

7. To make the filling, whip the cream until stiff peaks form and then set aside. Beat the cream cheese with a mixer until smooth. Add the sugar, vanilla and salt and beat through. Add the sour cream and whipped cream and whisk through for at least 2 minutes.

8. Pour the filling over the crust. Place in the refrigerator to chill for at least 2 hours.

9. Remove the springfrom casing, then pour the topping over the pie.

10. Decorate with the remaining raspberries and dust with icing sugar before serving.

RHUBARB AND SAFFRON CREAM TARTLETS

INGREDIENTS

Cases

170g (6oz) unsalted butter, room temperature

1 cup (220g, 8oz) caster sugar

1 tsp vanilla extract

1½ cups (185g, 6oz) plain flour

Filling

750g (1½ lb) rhubarb, cut into 2cm (1in) lengths

½ cup (110g, 4oz) plus 2 tbsps caster sugar

2 tbsps plain flour

Pinch of salt

1 cup (250ml, 8fl oz) full cream milk

3 eggs, room temperature

4 strands saffron, soaked in 1 tbsp warm water

½ tsp vanilla extract

METHOD

1. To start, toss the rhubarb with the 2 tablespoons of sugar in a large bowl until the pieces are evenly coated. Transfer the sugary rhubarb to a colander and place over a bowl. The rhubarb will drip out liquid – let it sit for at least 4 hours, preferably overnight.

2. To make the cases, preheat the oven to 190°C (375°F, Gas Mark 5) and grease six mini quiche tins.

3. Beat together the butter, sugar and vanilla with a mixer until it resembles whipped cream then mix the flour through.

4. Roll out on a floured surface until about 3mm (⅛ in) thick. Cut into six circles and fit them into the quiche tins. Prick the cases lightly with a fork. Line them with foil and fill with baking beads or uncooked rice. Bake for 20 minutes or until the edge is lightly browned. Remove the beads and foil and let them cool for at least 30 minutes.

5. Meanwhile make the filling, by whisking together the ½ cup of sugar with the flour and salt. Add a slug or two of milk, whisking until the mixture is nearly a batter. Add the remaining milk, eggs, saffron liquid and vanilla, whisking until just combined.

6. Gently press the rhubarb into the sieve with a fork to remove a bit more liquid and divide the pieces between the six quiche tins. Pour the freshly whisked custard over the rhubarb.

7. Bake until the custard is set and just browned on the edges for 25 minutes. Remove from the oven and let cool for at least 1 hour before serving.

GINGERBREAD PLUM SLICE

INGREDIENTS

250g (9oz) unsalted butter, chilled and cubed

1 cup (150g, 5oz) light brown sugar

2½ cups (300g, 10oz) almond meal

1¼ cups (140g, 5oz) plain flour, plus an extra ¼ cup (25g, 1oz)

¼ cup (75g, 3oz) golden syrup

2 large eggs, room temperature

1½ tbsps ground ginger

1 tsp allspice

1 tsp baking powder

1 cup (80g, 3oz) rolled oats

6 plums, stoned and chopped into slices

METHOD

1. Preheat the oven to 180°C (350°F, Gas Mark 4) and line a 20 x 30cm (8 x 12in) slice tin with greased baking paper.

2. Place butter, sugar and almond meal into a food processor and pulse until the mixture resembles lumpy breadcrumbs. Spoon out half the mix into a separate bowl and set aside.

3. Add the 1¼ cups flour and golden syrup into the mix in the processor and whizz until it just forms a dough. Pour the dough into the slice tin and smooth it all down with the back of a spoon. Bake for 20 mins until browned. Remove and let it cool in the tin for at least 15 minutes.

4. To make the filling, put the reserved almond mix back into the processor. Mix through the eggs, the ¼ cup flour, ginger, allspice and baking powder and whizz to a soft batter. Then stir in the rolled oats.

5. Place half the plums over the cooked base and then pour the mixture over the top. Push the remaining plums into the top of the mix.

6. Bake for 40 minutes. Let cool before cutting into desired squares.

CHERRY CLAFOUTIS

INGREDIENTS

3 cups (600g, 1lb 5oz) cherries, destoned (preferably fresh, but can used preserved)

3 large eggs, room temperature

1 cup (250ml, 8fl oz) full cream milk, room temperature

½ cup (110g, 4oz) caster sugar

1 tsp vanilla extract

1 tsp lemon zest

Pinch of salt

½ cup (60g, 2oz) plain flour, sifted

METHOD

1. Preheat the oven to 190°C (375°F, Gas Mark 5) and grease a heavy 25cm (10in) oven-proof deep frying pan.

2. Arrange the cherries in a single layer in the frying pan and put to one side.

3. Whisk together the eggs, milk, sugar, vanilla, lemon zest and salt together in a large mixing bowl until smooth for about 5 minutes.

4. Whisk in the flour until just mixed through. Pour the batter over the cherries, then bake for at least 30 minutes until golden brown on top and set.

5. Let it cool for 15 minutes, then serve hot with cream, custard or ice cream of your choice.

VICTORIA SPONGE CAKE

INGREDIENTS

Sponge

225g (8oz) unsalted butter, room temperature

1 cup (225g, 8oz) caster sugar

1¾ cups (225g, 8oz) plain flour

4 tsps baking powder

1 tsp salt

½ tsp vanilla extract

4 large eggs, room temperature

Cream

3 cups (750ml, 24fl oz) thickened cream

½ cup (115g, 4oz) caster sugar

½ tsp vanilla extract

To decorate

1 cup (200g, 7oz) fresh strawberries, halved

½ cup (60g, 2oz) fresh raspberries

1 cup (200g, 7oz) fresh cherries

Mint leaves

METHOD

1. To make the sponge, preheat the oven to 180°C (350°F, Gas Mark 4) and grease and flour two 23cm (9in) cake tins.

2. In a mixer, beat the butter and sugar together until it resembles whipped cream.

3. Sift the flour twice with the baking powder and salt. Add to the butter mixture in thirds until just mixed in. Mix in the vanilla and then add the eggs one at a time, completely mixing each one in before adding the next. Beat for a further 2 minutes until the mixture is smooth and light. Divide the mixture between the two cake tins.

4. Bake for 25 minutes until cooked or until a skewer inserted into the middle comes out clean. Let them cool in the tins for at least 2 minutes before turning out onto a wire rack. Let cool for at least 1 hour before assembling cake.

5. Whisk the cream together with the sugar until soft peaks form. Mix through the vanilla.

6. Spread one third of the cream in an even layer on top of one of the sponges. Place the second sponge on top and spread the rest of the cream over the top.

7. Arrange the strawberries, raspberries and cherries on top along with a couple of mint leaves.

LEMON POSSET

INGREDIENTS

2½ cups (600ml, 21fl oz) double cream

⅔ cup (140g, 5oz) caster sugar

2 large lemons, juiced and zested into thin strips

METHOD

1. Add the cream and sugar to a medium saucepan and heat over medium-hight heat until boiling. Reduce heat to medium-low and simmer for 5 minutes, stirring until the sugar is dissolved.

2. Remove the pot from the heat and stir through the lemon juice.

3. Divide the cream between 6 dessert glasses, then cover each with plastic wrap and place in the refrigerator to chill for at least 3 hours.

4. Serve garnished with lemon zest strips.

LEMON CURD

INGREDIENTS

1 cup (250ml, 8fl oz) fresh lemon juice

1½ tbsps lemon zest, finely grated

1 cup (220g, 8oz) caster sugar

160g (6oz) unsalted butter, chilled and chopped into 1cm (½ in) cubes

5 medium eggs, plus 2 egg yolks

METHOD

1. Whisk together the juice, zest, sugar and butter in a large heatproof bowl. Place the bowl over a pot of simmering water. Gently stir the mixture until the butter has melted.

2. Lightly whisk together the eggs and egg yolks. Pour one-quarter of the butter mixture into the eggs and stir through. Then whisk the egg mixture slowly back into the butter mixture.

3. Heat the curd for 10-15 minutes, stirring every couple of minutes until the mixture is thick and creamy.

4. Remove from the heat and let cool, gently stirring every now and then. Keep in a sealed container in the refrigerator until ready to use.

RED WINE POACHED PEAR TART

INGREDIENTS

Pastry case

150g (5oz) unsalted butter, chilled and cubed

¾ cup (125g, 4oz) dark brown sugar

3 large egg yolks

2½ cups (300g, 10oz) plain flour

1 tsp cinnamon

¼ tsp allspice

2 tbsps cold water

Custard filling

3 tbsps plain flour

½ cup (110g, 4oz) caster sugar

3 eggs, room temperature

1 tsp vanilla extract

⅔ cup (160ml, 5fl oz) milk

Pears

5 small Buerre Bosc pears

1 cinnamon stick

1 star anise

⅔ cup (100g, 3oz) light brown sugar

2½ cups (600ml, 21fl oz) red wine

¼ cup (30g, 1oz) almonds, roughly chopped

METHOD

1. To make the pastry case, beat the butter and sugar together until it resembles whipped cream. Then add the egg yolks one at a time, completely mixing each one in before adding the next.

2. Sift the flour with the cinnamon and allspice and then add to the butter mixture in thirds, mixing thoroughly each time. Add the water a small amount at a time until the mixture comes together to form a dough. Form the dough into a flattened disc, wrap in plastic wrap and chill in the fridge for at least 30 minutes.

3. Preheat the oven to 180°C (350°F, Gas Mark 4) and grease a 13 x 36cm (14 x 5in) rectangular flan tin.

4. Peel, halve and core the pears, keeping the stems intact. Place them in a heavy-based saucepan with the cinnamon stick, anise, sugar and wine. Bring to a boil, reduce heat to low, then cook, covered, for 30 minutes.

5. Roll out the pastry on a lightly floured board into a large rectangle to fit the flan tin. Carefully lift up and into the tin and trim off any excess pastry. Line with foil and baking beads or uncooked rice. Blind bake for 13 minutes, then remove the beads and foil and bake for a further 7 minutes. Let cool for at least 30 minutes before filling.

6. To make the custard, turn down the oven to to 160°C (325°F, Gas Mark 3). Then whisk flour, sugar and eggs together in a large mixing bowl. Stir in vanilla. Add milk, mixing until well combined. Skim off any bubbles then pour into the pastry case.

7. Bake the tart for 30 minutes until the filling is almost set. Remove the pears from the saucepan and gently push into the custard. Bake for a further 15 minutes.

8. Remove from the oven and let cool for 15 minutes. Drizzle the pear sauce over the top and sprinkle with the chopped almonds.

BAKEWELL TART

INGREDIENTS

175g (6oz) unsalted butter, chilled and chopped into 1cm (½ in) cubes

2 cups (440g, 1lb) caster sugar

3 large eggs, room temperature

1½ cups (185g, 6oz) plain flour

1 tsp baking powder

Pinch of salt

½ cup (60g, 2oz) almond meal

½ tsp vanilla extract

2 tbsps orange zest

¼ cup (60ml, 2fl oz) milk

360g (13oz) fresh or frozen cranberries, reserve ¼ cup for decoration

¼ cup (80g, 3oz) raspberry jam

½ cup (60g, 2oz) flaked almonds

2 tbsps icing sugar

METHOD

1. Preheat the oven to 180°C (350°F, Gas Mark 4) and grease a 25cm (10in) fluted pie dish.

2. In a large mixing bowl, beat the butter and sugar together until it resembles whipped cream. Add the eggs one at a time, completely mixing each one in before adding the next.

3. Sift together the flour, baking powder and salt and add to the butter mixture in thirds, along with the almond meal, ensuring each portion is just mixed through before adding the next.

4. Mix in the vanilla, zest and milk and stir to combine until smooth.

5. Pour half the cake mix into the pie dish. Stir together the cranberries with the jam and dot them around on the cake mix in the dish. Gently pour the rest of the batter over the top.

6. Bake for 1 hour until golden on top or until a skewer inserted into the middle comes out clean.

7. Let the cake cool in the dish for 15 minutes before turning out onto a wire rack. Sprinkle the almonds over the top of the tart and arrange the leftover cranberries on top then dust with icing sugar.

FENNEL ROASTED FRUITS

INGREDIENTS

8 medium yellow plums, stoned and halved

8 purple figs, halved

2 tbsps light brown sugar

1 tbsp coriander seeds

½ tbsp fennel seeds

1 tsp allspice

½ tsp ground cardamom

⅓ cup (115g, 4oz) honey

½ cup (125ml, 4fl oz) water

METHOD

1. Preheat the oven to 180°C (350°F, Gas Mark 4) and lightly grease a 23cm (9in) deep pie dish.

2. Arrange the plum and fig halves, cut side up, in the pie dish.

3. Toss the sugar together with the coriander seeds, fennel seeds, allspice and cardamom and then sprinkle the mixture over the fruit halves.

4. Drizzle over the honey and then pour the water over everything.

5. Bake for 40 minutes until the fruit is cooked through and the liquid is a thick syrup.

6. Serve the fruit hot with cream, custard or ice cream of your choice.

LEMON CREAM CAKE

INGREDIENTS

Cake

125g (4oz) butter, room temperature

1 cup (220g, 8oz) caster sugar

3 large eggs, room temperature

2 tbsps lemon zest

1 tbsp lemon juice

1½ cups (185g, 6oz) plain flour

1½ tsps baking powder

½ cup (125ml, 4fl oz) Greek yoghurt

Icing

300g (10oz) cream cheese, room temperature

150g (5oz) unsalted butter, room temperature

3 cups (465g, 15oz) icing sugar, sifted

3 tbsps freshly squeezed lemon juice

¼ cup lemon zest

1 tsp vanilla extract

Pinch of salt

To decorate

1 cup (250ml, 8fl oz) thickened cream

2 tsps caster sugar

2 slices lemon, quartered

METHOD

1. To make the cake, preheat the oven to 180°C (350°F, Gas Mark 4) and line a 20cm (8in) springform cake tin with greased baking paper.

2. Beat the butter and sugar together until it resembles whipped cream. Add the eggs one at a time, completely mixing each one in before adding the next, then stir in the zest and lemon juice.

3. Sift together the flour and baking powder and add to the mixture in thirds, along with the yoghurt, ensuring each portion is just mixed through before adding the next. Whisk until smooth.

4. Pour into the cake tin and bake for 35 minutes or until a skewer inserted into the middle comes out clean. Turn out onto a wire rack to cool completely to room temperature.

5. To make the cream icing, beat the cream cheese and butter together for about 3 minutes until smooth and no lumps remain. Beat in the icing sugar, half the lemon juice, the lemon zest, vanilla and salt on low speed. Once the sugar begins to dissolve, increase to high speed and beat for 3 minutes. Add the remaining lemon juice to make it thinner if needed.

6. Use a large serrated knife to cut the cake in half. Ice the bottom half with a quarter of the icing mixture then flip over the other cake half and place it on top. Evenly coat the cake over the top and sides with the icing.

7. To decorate, whip the cream with the caster sugar until stiff peaks form. Pipe small flourishes around the edge of the cake and top with the quartered lemon slices.

8. Refrigerate the cake for at least 40 minutes, then let it sit for 20 minutes outside the fridge before serving.

RHUBARB MERINGUE CAKE

INGREDIENTS

700g (1½ lb) rhubarb, cut into 2cm (1in) lengths

1 cup (215g, 8oz) caster sugar

200g (7oz) unsalted butter, room temperature

½ tsp vanilla extract

3 eggs, room temperature

1 cup (250ml, 8fl oz) Greek yoghurt

¼ cup (60ml, 2fl oz) full cream milk

3 cups (375g, 12oz) plain flour, sifted

½ tsp baking powder

½ portion of meringue topping (see recipe page 34)

METHOD

1. Preheat oven to 170°C (340°F, Gas Mark 4). Line a square 24cm (9½ in) cake tin and a large baking tray with baking paper.

2. Toss rhubarb with ¼ cup of the sugar and spread in a single layer on baking tray. Bake for 30 mins then remove from the oven and set aside to cool. Increase temperature to 180°C (350°F, Gas Mark 4).

3. Beat butter, remaining sugar and vanilla together in a large mixing bowl until it resembles whipped cream. Mix in the eggs one at a time. Stir the yoghurt and milk together then add with the flour and baking powder in thirds to the batter, ensuring each portion is just mixed through before adding the next. Spoon half the cake batter evenly over the base of the cake tin. Top with the rhubarb in an even layer. Spoon over the remaining cake batter. Bake for 45 minutes or until a skewer inserted into the centre comes out clean. Remove from oven and turn out onto a wire rack to cool for at least 1 hour. Cut into squares.

4. Spoon the prepared meringue filling into a piping bag and pipe a small amount on top of the squares in a wave pattern. Use a kitchen torch to brown the meringue tops.

SPICED STEWED RHUBARB

INGREDIENTS

500g (1lb 2oz) rhubarb, cut into 3cm (1in) lengths

⅓ cup (50g, 2oz) light brown sugar

1 tsp allspice

2 tbsps orange juice

2 tbsps Cointreau

2 cinnamon sticks

2 star anise

1 vanilla bean

METHOD

1. Toss the rhubarb together with the sugar and allspice in a medium saucepan. Add the orange juice, cinnamon sticks, star anise and vanilla bean.

2. Turn heat to medium, cover and cook for 15 minutes or until the rhubarb is tender.

3. Turn off the heat and let sit for 15 minutes.

4. Remove the cinnamon, anise and vanilla bean before serving.

SUMMER FRUITS TART

INGREDIENTS

Base

170g (6oz) unsalted butter, room temperature

1 cup (220g, 8oz) caster sugar

1 tsp vanilla extract

1½ cups (185g, 6oz) plain flour

Filling

¾ cup (165g, 6oz) caster sugar

2 tbsps arrowroot flour

Pinch of salt

¾ cup (185ml, 6fl oz) thickened cream

2 tbsps orange juice

3 large eggs, lightly beaten

Topping

1 tbsp cherry conserve

¼ cup (55g, 2oz) caster sugar

1 tbsp arrowroot flour

¼ cup (60ml, 2fl oz) water

3 cups (375g, 13oz) mixed fresh fruit (blueberries, raspberries, cherries, cranberries, etc)

METHOD

1. To make the base, preheat the oven to 190°C (375°F, Gas Mark 5) and grease a 23cm (9in) pie dish.

2. Beat together the butter, sugar and vanilla with a mixer until it resembles whipped cream then mix the flour through.

3. Press the mixture into bottom and sides of the pie dish. Prick lightly all over with a fork. Line with foil and fill with baking beads or uncooked rice. Bake for 25 minutes or until the edge is lightly browned. Remove the beads and foil and let cool for at least 30 minutes.

4. Reduce the oven to 160°C (325°F, Gas Mark 3).

5. Whisk together the sugar, arrowroot and salt. Add the cream, juice and eggs and whisk thoroughly until everything is thoroughly combined. Pour into the pastry case and bake for 30 minutes. Let cool for at least 2 hours.

6. To make the topping, heat the cherry conserve, sugar, flour and water in a small saucepan over medium heat until almost simmering. Stir until thickened, adding more water as needed until it forms a thick syrup. Remove from the heat and let cool for 15 minutes.

7. Gently stir the syrup through the berries and place on top of the custard.

PANNA COTTA WITH ORANGE JELLY

INGREDIENTS

Panna cotta

3 gold-strength gelatine leaves

1½ cups (375ml, 13fl oz) cream

½ cup (115g, 4oz) caster sugar

2¼ cups (560ml, 19 fl oz) Greek yoghurt

Orange jelly

2 gold-strength gelatine leaves

1 cup (250ml, 8fl oz) apple juice

1 tsp orange essence

2 tsps caster sugar

To decorate

1 large orange, peeled and sliced into 8 slices

8 sprigs of mint, to garnish

METHOD

1. To make the panna cotta, soak three gelatine leaves in a bowl of cold water for 5 minutes. Gently whisk together the cream and sugar in a medium saucepan over medium-high heat and bring slowly to the boil, stirring constantly, until sugar dissolves. Remove from heat. Squeeze the leaves to remove excess liquid and then whisk into the hot cream until dissolved. Strain the cream through a fine sieve into a large bowl and whisk in the yoghurt.

2. Pour the mixture into eight small dessert glasses about two-thirds of the way up. Chill in the refrigerator for at least 3 hours.

3. About 45 minutes before the panna cotta is ready, start making the jelly. Soak two gelatine leaves in cold water for 5 minutes. Heat the apple juice in a small pan over medium heat for 5 minutes and stir in the orange essence and sugar. Add gelatine leaves and whisk until dissolved. Remove from heat and cool for 30 minutes.

4. Pour the jelly on top of the panna cotta in each glass then chill in the refrigerator for 1 hour. Garnish with a slice of orange and sprig of mint.

APPLE AND ALMOND STRU- DEL

INGREDIENTS

800g (1¾ lb) red apples, peeled, cored and cut into 1cm (½ in) cubes

1 tbsp orange juice

1 tbsp brown sugar

2 tsps cinnamon

1 tsp allspice

16 large sheets filo pastry

225g (9oz) unsalted butter, melted

½ cup (60g, 2oz) almond meal

¼ cup (40g, 1½ oz) loosely packed brown sugar

¼ cup (40g, 1½ oz) sultanas

1 tsp cinnamon

1 tbsp icing sugar, to dust

3 tbsps flaked almonds, to decorate

METHOD

1. Preheat the oven to 200°C (400°F, Gas Mark 6) and line a large baking tray with baking paper.

2. Cook the apples, juice, brown sugar, cinnamon and allspice in a pan over medium heat for 15 minutes or until soft, stirring frequently. Drain apples over a sieve for at least 1 hour to remove excess liquid.

3. To assemble the strudel, place 1 sheet of filo pastry on a workbench. Lightly brush with melted butter. Repeat with remaining pastry sheets, placing one on top of the other.

4. Toss together the apple, almond meal, sugar, sultanas and cinnamon in a large mixing bowl. Spread the apple mixture slightly to one side along the filo sheets, lengthwise.

5. Tightly roll up the sheets and place the strudel, seam-side down, on the baking tray. Brush with remaining melted butter.

6. Bake for 25 minutes or until pastry is crisp and golden. Dust with icing sugar and sprinkle with flaked almonds. Serve warm or cold.

CRANBERRY CRUMBLE BITES

INGREDIENTS

Crumble topping

1 cup (125g, 4oz) self-raising flour

1 tsp ground cinnamon

¼ tsp allspice

75g (3oz) unsalted butter, chilled and cubed

½ cup (75g, 3oz) brown sugar

1 tbsp milk

Bases

125g (4oz) unsalted butter, chilled and cubed

½ cup (125g, 4oz) caster sugar

2 eggs, room temperature

1 cup (125g, 4oz) self-raising flour, sifted

2 tbsps icing sugar

Cranberries

3 tbsps unsalted butter

¼ cup (60ml, 2fl oz) water

1 tbsp lemon juice

¼ cup (55g, 2oz) caster sugar

2 cups (200g, 7oz) fresh cranberries

½ cup (155g, 5oz) agave syrup

METHOD

1. Preheat the oven to 180°C (350°F, Gas Mark 4) and lightly grease three 6-hole muffin tins. (These can be made a batch at a time, if needed.)

2. To make the crumble topping, sift the flour and spices into a food processor with the butter and pulse until the mixture resembles breadcrumbs.

3. Stir the brown sugar into the mix and then set the mix aside.

4. To make the bases, beat the butter and sugar together until it resembles whipped cream. Add the eggs one at a time, completely mixing each one in before adding the next.

5. Roughly mix in the flour. Divide half the batter between the 18 muffin tins.

6. Quickly stir the tablespoon of milk into the crumble mixture then place a dessertspoon of it on top of the batter mix.

7. Bake for 15-20 minutes until slightly browned on top. Leave for 5 minutes in the tin before turning out onto a wire rack to cool. Dust lightly with icing sugar.

8. To make the cranberry topping, melt the butter with the water, lemon juice and sugar in a small saucepan over medium heat. Heat until almost simmering and thickened.

9. Add the cranberries and gently stir them for 5 minutes, a few will split. Gently press them with a fork to squeeze out the juice.

10. Reduce the heat to low and keep stirring for 10 more minutes then stir in the agave syrup. Heat for a further 5 minutes. Remove from the heat and let cool for 30 minutes before using.

11. Dollop spoonfuls of the cranberries and syrup over each crumble bite. Serve.

VANILLA CHEESECAKE WITH STRAWBERRY SAUCE

INGREDIENTS

Base

115g (4oz) unsalted butter, room temperature

¼ cup (55g, 2oz) caster sugar

1 tsp vanilla extract

1 cup (125g, 4oz) plain flour

Filling

1¼ cups (300ml, 10fl oz) thickened cream

750g (1½ lb) cream cheese, room temperature, roughly chopped

¾ cup (165g, 6oz) caster sugar

2 tbsps arrowroot flour

4 large eggs, room temperature

2 tbsps vanilla extract

Strawberry sauce

2½ cups (500g, 1lb 2oz) fresh strawberries, hulled and roughly chopped

½ cup (110g, 4oz) caster sugar

½ tsp vanilla extract

1 tbsp lemon juice

METHOD

1. Preheat the oven to 190°C (375°F, Gas Mark 5) and line the bottom of a 23cm (9in) springform cake tin.

2. To make the base, beat together the butter, sugar and vanilla until it resembles whipped cream, then mix the flour through. Press the mixture into the cake tin. Prick lightly all over with a fork. Bake for 25 minutes or until the edge is lightly browned.

3. To make the filling, whip half the cream until stiff peaks form – do not over-whip – and set aside.

4. In a separate mixing bowl, beat the cream cheese until light and fluffy, then beat in the sugar and arrowroot until smooth. Beat in the eggs, one at a time, completely mixing each one in before adding the next. Then beat in the rest of the thickened cream and vanilla. Use a slotted spoon to gently fold in the whipped cream. Pour into the cake base.

5. Reduce the oven to 150°C (300°F, Gas Mark 2) and bake for 70 minutes or until the centre is almost set. Remove from oven and run a knife around the edge of the pan but let it cool in the pan on a rack. Refrigerate until chilled, for at least 4 hours, preferably overnight.

6. To make the strawberry sauce, place all the sauce ingredients in a saucepan over medium-high heat. Bring to a boil, stirring constantly, then reduce heat and simmer for 5 minutes. Remove from the heat then mash to puree the strawberries. Push the mixture through a sieve to extract the liquid. Return the liquid to a small saucepan and simmer for 3 minutes over medium heat. Skim off any foam. Cool for at least 15 minutes. Add half the pulp from the sieve back in to thicken it up if desired.

7. Serve the cheesecake with the sauce drizzled over the top.

PEACH AND SOUR CREAM CUSTARD PIE

INGREDIENTS

1 pre-cooked 23cm (9in) tart case (see recipe page 116)

Filling

¾ cup (165g, 6oz) caster sugar

2 tbsps arrowroot flour

Pinch of salt

¾ cup (185ml, 6fl oz) sour cream

2 tbsps orange juice

3 large eggs, lightly beaten

3 small peaches, stoned and sliced

Sprigs of mint, to garnish

METHOD

1. To make the filling, whisk together the sugar, arrowroot and salt. Add the sour cream, juice and eggs and whisk until everything is thoroughly combined. Pour into the pastry case.

2. Arrange the peach slices in the custard. Bake for 40 minutes or until the custard is set. Let cool for at least 2 hours before serving.

3. Serve topped with sprigs of mint.

HONEY GRILLED PEACHES AND CREAM

INGREDIENTS

1 cup (250ml, 8fl oz) Greek yogurt

¼ tsp vanilla extract

4 large ripe peaches, halved and stoned

¼ tsp cinnamon

¼ cup (90g, 3oz) honey

Sprigs of mint, to garnish

METHOD

1. Combine yogurt and vanilla and set aside

2. Lightly grease a large grill pan with butter and put over high heat.

3. Sprinkle the cut side of the peaches with cinnamon, then grill the peach halves for 5 minutes, cut side down. Turn them over and grill for another 5 minutes.

4. Serve the peaches hot, drizzled with honey and with a portion of the vanilla yoghurt and garnished with fresh mint leaves.

CRANBERRY LOAF CAKE WITH PINK ICING

INGREDIENTS

1²/₃ cups (205g, 7oz) plain flour

Pinch of salt

½ tsp baking powder

115g (4oz) unsalted butter, chilled cubed

1½ cups (330g, 12oz) caster sugar

½ cup (110g, 4oz) mascarpone, room temperature

1 tsp lemon zest

1 tsp vanilla extract

3 large eggs, room temperature

½ cup (125ml, 4fl oz) thickened cream

2 cups (200g, 7oz) fresh cranberries (can use frozen)

3 tbsps dried cranberries

Icing

¾ cup (120g, 4oz) packed icing sugar

1¾ tsps cranberry juice

Pinch of salt

2 tbsps icing sugar, to dust

METHOD

1. Preheat the oven to 180°C (350°F, Gas Mark 4) and butter and lightly dust with flour a 22 x 12 x 8cm (10 x 5 x 3in) loaf tin.

2. Sift together the flour, salt and baking powder and set aside.

3. In a large mixing bowl, beat the butter and sugar together until it resembles whipped cream. Add the mascarpone, lemon zest and vanilla and beat until fully incorporated. Add the eggs one at a time, completely mixing each one in before adding the next. Then mix through the cream.

4. Add the flour mixture in thirds, ensuring each portion is just mixed through before adding the next. Gently fold half the fresh cranberries and all of the dried cranberries into the cake mixture.

5. Pour the cake mix into the loaf tin and bake for 60 minutes or until a skewer inserted into the middle comes out clean. Let the cake cool in the tin for 15 minutes before turning out onto a wire rack.

6. To make the icing, whisk together the icing sugar, cranberry juice and salt until combined. Add more liquid as needed to make runny.

7. While the cake is still warm, drizzle the icing over the top and decorate with the rest of the cranberries.

8. Dust with the icing sugar and chill in the fridge for at least 1 hour until the icing is set.

FROZEN

SERVES 8-10 ★ PREP 20MIN (PLUS FREEZING) ★ COOK TIME 5MIN

ROCKY ROAD ICE-CREAM CAKE

INGREDIENTS

Base

1 packet ginger snap biscuits

140g (5oz) unsalted butter, melted

Filling

4 cups (1L, 2pt) chocolate ice cream, softened

3 cups (140g, 5oz) mini marshmallows

1½ cups (185g, 6oz) macadamia nuts, roughly chopped

1½ cups (235g, 8oz) dark chocolate chips

Topping

½ cup (125ml, 4fl oz) chocolate sauce, (see recipe page 16)

¾ cup (120g, 4oz) caramel chocolate chips (or white if you can't find caramel)

Sprigs of mint, to garnish

METHOD

1. To make the base, preheat the oven to 180°C (350°F, Gas Mark 4) and lightly grease a 23cm (9in) springform cake tin.

2. Use a food processor to break up the biscuits into crumbs. Pour in the butter and pulse a couple of times to combine. Press the mixture into the bottom and the sides of the cake tin. Bake for 15 minutes, then remove from the oven and chill in the fridge for at least 30 minutes.

3. Mix the ice cream together with 2 cups of marshmallows, 1 cup of chopped macadamia nuts and 1 cup of the chocolate chips. Spoon into the biscuit base and place in the freezer for at least 3 hours until frozen.

4. Heat the chocolate sauce in a small saucepan over medium heat for 5 minutes.

5. Remove the cake from the freezer and top with the remaining marshmallows, nuts and chocolate chips as well as the caramel chocolate chips.

6. Drizzle the warm chocolate sauce over the top and garnish with mint leaves. Serve immediately.

PINEAPPLE AND GINGER CREME FRAICHE ICE CREAM

INGREDIENTS

1 cup (200g, 7oz) fresh pineapple pieces

¾ cup (200ml, 7fl oz) full cream milk

¾ cup (175g, 6oz) caster sugar

600g (1lb 5oz) creme fraiche

1 tbsp fresh ginger, grated

¼ cup (10g, ¼ oz) fresh coriander, roughly chopped

METHOD

1. Place the pineapple pieces in a small blender container and give it a couple of pulses to break it up a bit more. Pour into a sieve and let it drain for 1 hour. Squeeze the pulp gently to release a bit more of the liquid. Keep the pulp.

2. Whisk together the milk, sugar, creme fraiche, ginger and coriander. Set aside for 10 mins for the sugar to melt.

3. Gently stir through the pineapple pulp. Then place in an ice-cream machine and churn for at least 30 minutes until thickened.

4. Transfer the ice cream to an airtight container and place in the freezer. Freeze for at least 4 hours, preferably overnight.

5. Serve with fresh slices of pineapple and a couple of coriander leaves.

MATCHA MINT POPS

INGREDIENTS

1 portion matcha green tea ice cream, softened (see recipe page 170)

¼ cup (10g, ¼ oz) fresh mint, finely chopped

¼ cup (40g, 1½ oz) chia seeds

METHOD

1. Place the matcha ice cream in a large bowl and beat the mint and chia seeds through it until completely combined.

2. Spoon the ice cream into eight icy-pole moulds and insert a paddle pop stick halfway into each.

3. Place in the freezer and freeze for at least 4 hours, preferably overnight.

4. Unmould and serve chilled.

SERVES 8-10 ★ PREP 30min (PLUS FREEZING)

BERRY ICE-CREAM CAKE

INGREDIENTS

Base

200g (7oz) butternut snap
biscuits

100g (3½ oz) unsalted
butter, melted

Filling

8 cups (2L, 4pt) vanilla
ice-cream, softened (use
good quality)

1¼ cups (250g, 9oz) fresh
strawberries, washed and
hulled

1¾ cups (200g, 7oz)
frozen raspberries

2 cups (200g, 7oz) fresh
blueberries

Topping

2 cups (250g, 9oz)
fresh summer berries
to decorate (cherries,
raspberries, strawberries,
blueberries, etc)

METHOD

1. Roughly chop the fruit for the filling into small pieces and use paper towels to soak up excess liquid. Place in the freezer and chill for at least 1 hour before using.

2. To make the base, preheat the oven to 180°C (350°F, Gas Mark 4) and line a 23cm (9in) springform cake tin with plastic wrap.

3. Use a food processor to break up the biscuits into crumbs. Pour in the butter and pulse a couple of times to combine. Press the mixture into the bottom of the cake tin. Bake for 15 minutes, then remove from the oven and chill in the freezer for at least 30 minutes.

4. Place the ice cream into a large mixing bowl. Add the chilled chopped fruit and blend through the ice cream.

5. Spread the ice cream over the biscuit base in the cake tin. Try not to have any air pockets. Flatten the top, then create a depression in the middle to hold the fruit when it's ready to serve.

6. Cover with plastic wrap and freeze for at least 4 hours, preferably overnight.

7. Before serving, remove the cake from the tin and top with the 2 cups of fresh summer fruit.

FREAKSHAKE

INGREDIENTS

1 cup (250ml, 8fl oz) chocolate sauce (see recipe page 16)

2 cups (500ml, 1pt) milk

½ cup (125ml, 4fl oz) caramel cream (see recipe page 19)

2 arrowroot biscuits

8-10 mini meringue drops

¼ cup (40g, 1½ oz) coloured sprinkles

Cream topping

1½ cups (375ml, 13fl oz) thickened cream

½ tbsp caster sugar

¼ tsp vanilla extract

Chocolate magic topping

½ cup (125ml, 4fl oz) chocolate magic topping (see recipe page 96)

METHOD

1. Whip the cream for the cream topping with the sugar and vanilla until stiff peaks form. Chill in the refrigerator until ready to use.

2. Warm the chocolate sauce and place in a squirt sauce bottle and squirt generously around the sides of two mason jars.

3. Fill each jar three-quarters full with milk. Spoon the whipped cream over the milk to create two small mountains of whipped cream.

4. Use a flat knife or spatula to smear the caramel sauce around the top third of each jar.

5. Break up the arrowroot biscuits into small pieces and press into the caramel of one jar, with a couple of meringue drops. Gently press a couple of meringue drops into the cream on top of the other jar.

6. Press sprinkles into the caramel cream of the undecorated jar and sprinkle a few on the top of the undecorated cream on the other jar.

7. Gently warm the chocolate magic topping and drizzle over the top of both shakes.

8. Insert a paper straw into both and serve.

CHOC POPS

INGREDIENTS

1¼ cups (300ml, 10fl oz) caramel ice cream, softened

1⅔ cups (400ml, 13fl oz) chocolate ice cream, softened

1¼ cups (300ml, 10fl oz) mocha ice cream, softened

METHOD

1. Place small portions of each ice cream in layers into ten icy-pole moulds until each mould is filled.

2. Place a paddle pop stick halfway into each.

3. Place in the freezer and freeze for at least 4 hours, preferably overnight.

4. Unmould and serve chilled.

CHOCOLATE PARFAIT

INGREDIENTS

250g (9oz) dark cooking chocolate

8 large egg yolks, room temperature

1¾ cups (250g, 9oz) light brown sugar

⅓ cup (100g, 4oz) agave syrup

100g (3½ oz) unsalted butter, room temperature

1 cup (100g, 4oz) cacao powder

1¼ cups (300ml, 10fl oz) double cream

Vanilla cream

1¼ cups (300ml, 10fl oz) whipping cream

1 tbsp caster sugar

¼ tsp vanilla paste

METHOD

1. Line a 25 x 15 x 7cm (10 x 6 x 3in) loaf tin with plastic wrap. (Try to make it as smooth as you can.)

2. Melt 150g of the chocolate in a heatproof bowl over a pot of simmering water. Once melted, remove from the heat and set aside to cool for 15 minutes. Whisk together the egg yolks, brown sugar and agave in a separate bowl, stir in ¼ cup of chocolate, then gently whisk the egg mixture back into the chocolate mix.

3. Return the bowl to sit over the simmering pot and stir for 4 minutes until it has thickened. Whisk in the butter and cacao until mixed through. Remove the bowl from the heat and let cool for at least 1 hour.

4. Whip the double cream until stiff peaks form, then use a slotted spoon to gently fold it into the chocolate mixture.

5. Shave the remaining cooking chocolate into small shards and stir into the parfait mix. Spoon into the loaf tin, trying not to create any air pockets.

6. Freeze for at least 4 hours, preferably overnight.

7. Gently whip the cream with the caster sugar and vanilla paste until it thickens slightly but is still pourable.

8. Serve the parfait with the vanilla cream.

CHERRY CHOC FUDGE POPS

INGREDIENTS

1 cup (250ml, 8fl oz) milk, chilled

¾ cup (165g, 6oz) caster sugar

2 tsps vanilla extract

2 cups (500ml, 1pt) thickened cream

1 cup (200g, 7oz) fresh cherries, pitted and finely chopped

1 cup (155g, 5oz) dark chocolate, grated

1 cup (250ml, 8fl oz) caramel cream (see recipe page 19)

METHOD

1. Mix together the milk and sugar in a mixing bowl and whisk until the sugar is dissolved. Add the vanilla and cream.

2. Pour into an ice-cream maker and churn for 20 minutes. Add the cherries and ¾ cup of the grated chocolate. Churn for a further 5 minutes.

3. Fill ten icy-pole moulds with the ice-cream mix, place a paddle pop stick halfway into each one. Freeze for at least 4 hours, preferably overnight.

4. Line a large baking tray with baking paper. Dip the top quarters of each icy pole in the caramel sauce and use a small spatula to smear it further down. Lay each one on the baking paper and sprinkle with the remaining grated chocolate.

5. Freeze for one hour, then serve.

FROZEN STRAWBERRY BARK

INGREDIENTS

4 cups (1L, 2pt) Greek yogurt

¾ cup (235g, 8oz) agave syrup

3 cups (600g, 1lb 5oz) fresh strawberries, chopped

1 cup (155g, 5oz) mini dark chocolate chips

METHOD

1. Line the bottom and sides of a large deep-sided baking dish with baking paper

2. Add the yoghurt and agave to a large mixing bowl and whisk until combined.

3. Stir in the strawberries and chocolate chips.

4. Spread the mixture over the bottom of the baking dish.

5. Freeze for at least 4 hours, preferably overnight.

6. Use a knife to break up the frozen bark into small bite-size pieces and serve chilled.

SERVES 8 ★ PREP 40MIN (PLUS CHILLING) ★ COOK TIME 20MIN

BAKED ALASKA

INGREDIENTS

Sponge

4 large eggs, room temperature

²⁄₃ cup (140g, 5oz) caster sugar

²⁄₃ cup (80g, 3oz) plain flour

Pinch of salt

1½ tbsps unsalted butter, melted

½ tsp vanilla extract

1 tsp lemon zest

1 cup (250ml, 8fl oz) rum

Filling

1¼ cups (300ml, 10fl oz) vanilla ice cream, softened

1²⁄₃ cups (400ml, 13fl oz) strawberry ice cream, softened

2 cups (500ml, 1pt) chocolate ice cream, softened

Meringue

9 large egg whites, room temperature

1½ cups (330g, 12oz) caster sugar

2 tsps vanilla extract

To serve

1 cup (200g, 7oz) fresh strawberries, halved

METHOD

1. To make the sponge, preheat the oven to 160°C (325°F, Gas Mark 3) and line a 25cm (10in) round cake tin with baking paper.

2. Beat eggs and sugar together for about 5 minutes until thick, fluffy and pale. Sift in the flour and salt and beat until mixed thoroughly. Drizzle in the melted butter and again mix through completely. Pour into the cake pan and bake for 20 minutes or until a skewer inserted into the middle comes out clean. Let the cake cool to room temperature in the tin before the next step.

3. Use a large pudding-style bowl that holds around 10 cups volume. Line with plastic wrap. Use a large serrated knife to slice the cake into roughly 1cm (½ in) layers. Reserve one layer of the cake. Cut the rest into triangles, and fit them together to snugly line the bowl. (They don't have to be perfect but try not to leave any gaps.) Sprinkle the cake with ¼ cup of rum.

4. Place the vanilla ice cream in the bottom of the bowl, then layer the strawberry over the top and then the chocolate over that.

5. Cut a circle from the reserved piece of cake to fit on top of the chocolate layer so it is flush with the outside layer of cake and seals up the ice cream. Sprinkle a tablespoon or two of rum over this. Freeze for at least 2 hours, until the ice cream is hard.

6. To make the meringue, beat the egg whites until soft peaks form. Gradually beat in sugar for 5 minutes until glossy stiff peaks form.

7. Flip the cake over onto a serving dish so it is sitting in a dome shape. Coat the cake completely in the meringue, fluffing up the outside with your spatula to create a prickly effect. Place back in the freezer for another hour or two to chill.

8. Before serving, use a kitchen torch to brown the outside of the meringue. Serve with strawberries.

Optional: To serve, pour the rest of the rum in a flame-proof pouring jug and set it alight. Pour the flaming rum around the bottom of the meringue.

MANGO SORBET

INGREDIENTS

5 cups (825g, 1lb 12oz) mango flesh, roughly chopped

¼ cup (60ml, 2fl oz) water, chilled

¾ cup (165g, 6oz) caster sugar

1 tsp lemon juice

Pinch of salt

Fresh berries and mint leaves, to serve

METHOD

1. Add the mango and water to a blender and puree until smooth. Push through a fine wire sieve until you have 3 cups. Reserve the rest of the mango for other use.

2. Place the puree into a large mixing bowl and add the sugar, lemon juice and salt. Whisk together until the sugar is dissolved.

3. Pour the mixture into an ice-cream maker and churn for 30 minutes.

4. Transfer to an airtight container and freeze for at least 4 hours, preferably overnight.

5. Serve with fresh berries and mint leaves.

STRAWBERRY GRANITA

INGREDIENTS

½ cup (110g, 4oz) caster sugar

½ cup (125ml, 4fl oz) warm filtered water

1¼ cups (250g, 9oz) strawberries, hulled and chopped

½ cup (125ml, 4fl oz) pomegranate juice

2 tbsps lemon juice

4 sprigs of mint, to garnish

METHOD

1. Gently heat the sugar and water in a small saucepan over medium heat until the sugar is dissolved. Remove from heat and let cool to room temperature.

2. Puree the strawberries, then push through a sieve to remove seeds.

3. In a large mixing bowl, mix together the puree, pomegranate juice and lemon juice. Then add in the syrup, a quarter at a time. You may not need it all, add it to taste.

4. Spread the mixture out in a shallow dish and freeze for at least 4 hours, preferably overnight.

5. Use a fork to scrape up the granita mixture until light and fluffy.

6. Serve garnished with sprigs of mint.

MATCHA GREEN TEA ICE CREAM

INGREDIENTS

2 cups (500ml, 1pt) full cream milk

2 tbsps matcha green tea powder

1 cup (250ml, 8fl oz) thickened cream

6 egg yolks, room temperature

½ cup (120g, 4oz) caster sugar

½ tsp vanilla extract

Mint leaves, to garnish

METHOD

1. In a small mixing bowl add 75ml of milk and whisk in the matcha powder until it's mostly dissolved. Add this to a medium-sized saucepan with the rest of the milk.

2. Add half of the cream to the saucepan and heat over medium heat. Gently stir until almost simmering. Remove from heat and let cool, with the lid on, for 20 minutes.

3. In a separate mixing bowl, whisk together the rest of the cream, the egg yolks and the sugar. Slowly add the milk, gently whisking it through and taking care that it's cool enough not to cook the egg yolks.

4. Pour the mixture back into the saucepan and heat over medium heat until it's thick enough to coat the back of a spoon.

5. Remove the pot from the heat and place in a sink or container half-filled with ice water. Let it cool completely, stirring occasionally.

6. Transfer the mix to an ice-cream maker and churn for 30 minutes until thickened.

7. Scoop out into an airtight container and place in the freezer for at least 4 hours, preferably overnight.

8. Serve garnished with mint leaves.

NO-BAKE FROZEN RASPBER-RY CRUNCH CAKE

INGREDIENTS

Base

²/₃ cup (80g, 3oz) almonds, roughly chopped

²/₃ cup (80g, 3oz) walnuts, roughly chopped

¼ cup (20g, ¾ oz) desiccated coconut

1½ cups (260g, 9oz) Medjool dates, pitted and chopped

1 tbsp coconut oil

Filling

½ cup (60g, 2oz) sunflower seeds

2½ cups (310g, 10oz) fresh or frozen raspberries

1 x 400g (14oz) can coconut cream

¾ cup (60g, 2oz) shredded coconut

²/₃ cup (115g, 4oz) Medjool dates, pitted and chopped

Pinch of salt

2 tsps psyllium husk, ground

10 fresh raspberries, to garnish

METHOD

1. To make the base, mix all the base ingredients together in a large mixing bowl. Line a 20cm (8in) cake tin with baking paper and press the nut mix into the bottom in an even layer. Chill in the refrigerator for at least 30 minutes.

2. To make the filling, soak the sunflower seeds in water for at least 4 hours, then drain.

3. Place the raspberries, soaked sunflower seeds, coconut cream, coconut, dates and salt in a blender and blend until smooth. Then add in the psyllium husk to bind the mixture and again blend until thoroughlly mixed through.

4. Pour the filling into the cake tin. Place in the freezer for at least 4 hours, preferably overnight.

5. Remove the cake from the casing and arrange the fresh raspberries around the edge of the cake. Serve chilled.

HOMEMADE POMEGRANATE ICE CREAM

INGREDIENTS

1 cup (250ml, 8fl oz) of pomegranate juice

2 cups (500ml, 1pt) thickened cream

1 x 400g (14oz) can sweetened condensed milk

⅓ cup (70g, 2½ oz) caster sugar

3 medium limes, juiced

Seeds of 1 fresh pomegranate

METHOD

1. Mix together the juice, cream, condensed milk and sugar in a large mixing bowl.

2. Strain the lime juice and add to taste. The more you add, the tarter your ice cream will be.

3. Pour the mix into your ice cream maker and churn for 30 minutes until thickened.

4. Transfer to an airtight containter and freeze for at least 4 hours, preferably overnight.

5. Serve with fresh pomegranate seeds.

DARK CHOCOLATE AND PISTACHIO SEMIFREDDO

INGREDIENTS

½ cup (75g, 3oz) light brown sugar

4 medium eggs, room temperature

350g (12oz) dark cooking chocolate, roughly chopped

1¾ cups (450ml, 15fl oz) double cream

1 cup (125g, 4oz) pistachios, roughly chopped, reserve ¼ cup for garnish

METHOD

1. Line a 20 x 10cm (8 x 4in) loaf tin with lightly oiled plastic wrap — make sure you leave overhang.

2. Place the sugar and eggs in a heatproof heavy mixing bowl over a pot of simmering water and whisk them together for 5 minutes until pale and thickened to at least double the volume and the sugar has dissolved. Remove from heat and place in a sink or container with cold water.

3. Keep whisking until the mixture is lukewarm.

4. Melt 250g of the chocolate in a small heatproof mixing bowl over a pot of simmering water. Gently fold it into the egg mixture.

5. Whip the cream until peaks form. Gently mix the cream and pistachios into the chocolate mixture.

6. Spoon the mixture into the loaf tin, trying to avoid air pockets, and smooth it over. Cover with plastic wrap and freeze for at least 4 hours, preferably overnight.

7. Before serving, melt the rest of the chocolate in a small heatproof mixing bowl over a pot of simmering water.

8. Turn the loaf out of the tin and peel off the plastic. Warm the tin by placing in warm water and then replace the plastic wrap inside the tin. Working quickly, spread the melted chocolate in the bottom of the tin, then replace the loaf back inside, gently pushing it down to squash the melted chocolate down the sides.

9. Freeze for at least an hour, turn out the loaf again and gently peel off the plastic.

10. Serve chilled, garnished with the reserved pistachios.

FROZEN BLUEBERRY YOGHURT

INGREDIENTS

4 cups (400g, 14oz) frozen blueberries, reserve ¾ cup for garnish

2 cups (500ml, 1pt) Greek yoghurt

4 tbsps caster sugar

½ tsp lemon juice

Mint, to garnish

METHOD

1. Combine the blueberries, sugar and lemon juice in a medium saucepan. Bring to a simmer over medium heat. Reduce the heat to a gentle simmer, then cook, stirring occasionally, for 15 minutes.

2. Strain the mixture through a fine mesh sieve placed over a bowl. Push the blueberries with the back of a spoon to extract as much liquid as possible, then discard the mashed blueberries.

3. Transfer mixture to a tray and place in the freezer for 45 minutes, stirring every 10 minutes.

4. Stir the chilled blueberry mixture and chilled yogurt together, then freeze in an ice cream maker according to the manufacturer's instructions.

5. Transfer the frozen yogurt to the freezer for several hours for a scoopable consistency.

FROZEN BLUEBERRY CHEESECAKE

INGREDIENTS

1 cheesecake base (see recipe page 126)

2 cups (200g, 7oz) fresh or frozen blueberries

2 tbsps lemon juice

½ cup (180g, 6oz) honey

1½ cups (335g, 12oz) mascarpone cheese

1 cup (250ml, 8fl oz) Greek yoghurt

1 cup (100g, 3½ oz) fresh blueberries, to garnish

Sprigs of mint, to garnish

METHOD

1. Let the base cool to room temperature.

2. Blend together the blueberries, lemon juice and honey. Add to a large mixing bowl and stir together with the mascarpone and yoghurt. Pour it over the base.

3. Freeze for at least 4 hours, preferably overnight.

4. Before serving, remove from the cake tin and let soften for 20 minutes.

5. Serve with fresh blueberries and sprigs of mint.

THREE-LAYER FROZEN CHOCOLATE MOUSSE CAKE

INGREDIENTS

80g (3oz) dark cooking chocolate, roughly chopped

80g (3oz) white cooking choclate, roughly chopped

6 eggs, separated

²/₃ cup (150g, 5oz) caster sugar

2½ cups (600ml, 21fl oz) thickened cream, whipped

2 tbsps brewed espresso coffee, cooled

Berries, to decorate

¼ cup (125ml, 4fl oz) chocolate sauce (see recipe page 16)

METHOD

1. Line a 20 x 10cm (8 x 4in) loaf tin with lightly oiled plastic wrap – make sure you leave overhang.

2. Melt the dark chocolate and white chocolate in separate small heatproof mixing bowls over a pot of simmering water. Set aside.

3. Beat two of the egg yolks and a third of the sugar together for 5 minutes until they're pale and thickened to at least double the volume and the sugar has dissolved. Whisk in the melted dark chocolate until combined.

4. Beat two of the egg whites until soft peaks form and then fold into the chocolate mixture.

5. Use a slotted spoon to gently fold the chocolate mixture into one-third of the whipped cream. Spread it in the bottom of the loaf tin in a smooth layer.

6. Repeat steps 3-5 two more times, substituting the coffee and then the white chocolate instead of the dark chocolate.

7. Wrap over the top of the cake and freeze for at least 4 hours, preferably overnight.

8. Before serving, turn the cake out of the rin and remove the plastic wrap. Top with fruit of choice and drizzle over some of the chocolate sauce. Let side for 10 minutes to soften slightly.

ARCTIC ROLL

INGREDIENTS

Cake

3 medium eggs, room temperature

½ cup (100g, 4oz) caster sugar

1 tsp vanilla extract

¾ cup (100g, 3oz) plain flour

½ tsp baking powder

2 tbsps icing sugar

Filling

2 cups (500ml, 1pt) vanilla ice cream, softened

1½ cups (490g, 1lb 1oz) raspberry jam

METHOD

1. Preheat the oven to 200°C (400°F, Gas Mark 6) line a 23 x 33cm (9 x 13in) Swiss roll tin with greased baking paper.

2. Form the ice cream into a long log around 30cm (12in) in length. Place in the freezer while making the rest of the recipe.

3. Beat the eggs, sugar and vanilla together for 5 minutes until thickened and pale and at least doubled in volume. Sift the flour and baking powder into the mixture and gently whisk it through. then mix through 1 tablespoon of lukewarm water.

4. Spread the mixture evenly over the bottom of the tin. Bake for 12 minutes or until cooked through. Let cool for 15 minutes.

5. Lay out a sheet of baking paper, slightly larger than the tin and sprinkle the icing sugar over it. Turn out the sponge onto the dusted paper and let cool for a further 15 minutes.

6. Spread the jam in a layer over the cake, leaving a 3cm (1in) gap around the edges. Place the ice-cream log along the sponge slightly to one side. Roll up, peeling away the paper as you go.

7. Trim the ends flush with the ice cream and serve.

FROZEN LIME SOUFFLE

INGREDIENTS

1 cup (250ml, 8fl oz) water

6 large egg whites, room temperature

1 cup (230ml, 8fl oz) glucose syrup

2 cups (500ml, 1pt) thickened cream, chilled

1½ tbsps grated lime zest

1 tsp limoncello (optional)

8 thin slices of lime

METHOD

1. Cut out long rectangles of baking paper that you can secure around the tops of 8 dessert glasses or ramekins so that they sit about 4cm (1½ in) higher than the rims.

2. Beat the egg whites until soft peaks form. While continuing to beat, pour the glucose syrup in a thin stream down the side of the bowl into the egg whites. Beat until incorporated and stiff peaks form. Set aside.

3. Whip the cream with 1 teaspoon lime zest and limoncello until soft peaks form. Use a slotted spoon to gently fold in the beaten egg whites.

4. Spoon into the dessert glasses and about 2cm (1in) up the sides of the baking paper. Smooth the tops. Place in the freezer for at least 4 hours, preferably overnight.

5. Gently remove the baking paper from the glasses, sprinkle over some lime zest and garnish with a twisted slice of lime.

SUMMER FRUITS SEMIFRED-DO

INGREDIENTS

⅓ cup (70g, 2½ oz) caster sugar

1 tbsp honey

2 eggs, room temperature

4 medium egg yolks, room temperature

1⅔ cups (420ml, 14fl oz) double cream

1 tbsp rose water

1 tsp vanilla extract

1¼ cups (150g, 5oz) fresh raspberries

¾ cup (150g, 5oz) fresh strawberries, hulled and quartered

1½ cups (185g, 6oz) pistachios, chopped

METHOD

1. Line a 20 x 10cm (8 x 4in) loaf tin with plastic wrap, making sure you leave overhang.

2. Place the sugar, honey, eggs and egg yolks in a heavy mixing bowl over a pot of simmering water and whisk them together for 5 minutes until they're pale and thickened and the sugar is dissolved.

3. Remove the bowl from the heat and let cool for 20 minutes, whisking briefly every 10 minutes.

4. Whip the cream until stiff peaks form and fold into the egg mixture, along with the rose water and vanilla.

5. Spread one-third of the mixture on the bottom of the loaf tin.

6. In a separate bowl, mash together ¼ cup each of the raspberries and strawberries and mix through ⅓ cup of the pistachios. Layer this mixture over the cream and then gently pour the rest of the cream over the top.

7. Transfer to the freezer to firm up for at least 3 hours. Remove from the freezer and press the remaining berries and pistachios into the top.

8. Return to the freezer for another 3 hours.

9. When ready to serve, turn the semifreddo out onto a plate, remove the wrap and let it stand for 10 minutes to soften.

EASY

ROCKY ROAD

INGREDIENTS

125g (4oz) unsalted butter, room temperature

½ cup (110g, 4oz) caster sugar

3 tbsps Dutch cocoa

1 large egg, room temperature

250g (9oz) Marie biscuits, chopped

8 marshmallows (pink or white), chopped

²/₃ cup (80g, 3oz) peanuts, roughly chopped

Icing

1 cup (155g, 5oz) icing sugar

2 tbsps Dutch cocoa powder

2 tsps unsalted butter, melted

1 tbsp hot water

METHOD

1. Line a 20 x 20cm (8in) slice tin with baking paper.

2. Mix together the butter, sugar and cocoa in a small saucepan over medium heat. Once the butter is melted and everything is combined, remove from heat.

3. Whisk the egg into the chocolate mix until thoroughly combined. Mix through the biscuits, marshmallows and peanuts until they're evenly distributed.

4. Spread the mix into the slice tin – no need to smooth it out, leave it rough.

5. Whisk together the icing ingredients and pour over the top of the mixture. Smooth this over as evenly as you can.

6. Cover with plastic wrap and refrigerate for at least 4 hours, preferably overnight. Cut into 4cm (1½ in) squares and serve.

SKILLET COOKIE

INGREDIENTS

110g (4oz) unsalted butter, room temperature , plus extra for greasing

⅔ cup (150g, 5oz) caster sugar

1 large egg, room temperature

1 tsp vanilla extract

1⅔ cups (200g, 7oz) plain flour

¾ tsp bicarbonate of soda

Pinch of salt

200g (7oz) mini chocolate chips

METHOD

1. Preheat the oven to 180°C (350°F, Gas Mark 4) and grease an oven-proof frying pan with butter.

2. Beat the butter and sugar together until it resembles whipped cream. Mix in the egg and vanilla extract.

3. Sift together the flour, bicarb and salt then add to the batter and mix through thoroughly. Stir in the chocolate chips so they're evenly distributed throughout the batter.

4. Spread the batter evenly over the bottom of the frying pan.

5. Bake for 20 minutes or until golden brown on top.

6. Serve warm with whipped cream or ice cream.

VALENTINE WAFFLES

INGREDIENTS

Waffles

2 cups (250g, 8oz) self-raising flour

1 tbsp light brown sugar

½ tsp salt

½ tsp allspice

3 large eggs, separated, room temperature

2 cups (500ml, 1pt) full cream milk

¼ cup (60ml, 2fl oz) canola or vegetable oil

½ tsp vanilla extract

Topping

1¼ cups (300ml, 10fl oz) thickened cream

½ tbsp caster sugar

½ cup (160g, 6oz) strawberry jam

¾ cup (150g, 5oz) fresh strawberries, halved

⅓ cup (40g, 1½ oz) toasted walnuts

METHOD

1. In a large mixing bowl, stir together the flour, sugar, salt and allspice.

2. In a separate bowl, whisk together the egg yolks, milk, oil and vanilla until thoroughly combined.

3. Make a well in the flour and stir the wet ingredients in until just blended.

4. Beat the egg whites until stiff peaks form, then use a slotted spoon to gently fold them into the waffle batter.

5. Pour the batter into a waffle iron in small batches and cook as required until golden brown.

6. Whip the cream with the sugar until thickened.

7. For each serving, cut two waffles in half and spread one half of each generously with whipped cream and jam. Place the other half on top.

8. Serve topped with more cream and fresh strawberries and walnuts and drizzled with some more jam.

LEMON SURPRISE PUDDING

INGREDIENTS

50g (2oz) unsalted butter, room temperature

⅓ cup (80g, 3oz) caster sugar

3 tbsps lemon zest

3 tbsps lemon juice

1 cup (250ml, 8fl oz) full cream milk

2 large eggs, separated

2 tbsps plain flour

½ cup (50g, 2oz) fresh blueberries, to garnish

Sprigs of mint, to garnish

2 tbsps icing sugar, to dust

METHOD

1. Preheat the oven to 180°C (350°F, Gas Mark 4) and lightly butter four ramekins or dariole moulds.

2. Beat the butter and sugar together until it resembles whipped cream. Mix through the lemon zest and juice. Then whisk in the milk, egg yolks and flour.

3. Beat the egg whites until stiff peaks form. Use a slotted spoon to fold it into the lemon mixture then divide the batter evenly between the ramekins.

4. Place a tea towel in the bottom of a large deep baking dish and place the ramekins on top of the towel.

5. Fill the dish with enough water to come halfway up the sides of the ramekins.

6. Bake for 25 minutes until they've risen and are cooked on top.

7. Turn out onto serving bowls, top with a couple of blueberries, a mint sprig and dust with icing sugar.

CUSTARD COOKIE POTS

INGREDIENTS

1 batch warm custard (see recipe page 210)

4 Marie biscuits

1½ tbsps icing sugar

1 tsp nutmeg

METHOD

1. Pour the custard into four dessert glasses.

2. Gently place a Marie biscuit on top.

3. Cover with plastic wrap and place in the refrigerator to chill for 2 hours.

4. Remove the plastic wrap, dust each with the icing sugar and nutmeg and serve.

SERVES 6-8 ★ PREP 30MIN ★ COOK TIME 30MIN

POFFERTJES (DUTCH MINI PANCAKES)

INGREDIENTS

2 cups (250g, 8oz) plain flour

2 tsps baking powder

Pinch of salt

2 tbsps caster sugar

1 cup (250ml, 8fl oz) full cream milk

½ cup (125ml, 4fl oz) water

3 eggs, lightly beaten

150g (5oz) butter, room temperature

½ cup (80g, 3oz) icing sugar

1 cup (100g, 3½ oz) fresh blueberries , to garnish

Sprig lemon thyme, to garnish

METHOD

1. Sift the flour, baking powder and salt into a large mixing bowl. Stir through the caster sugar.
2. Add milk and water and whisk until combined.
3. Whisk in the eggs until thoroughly mixed through and you have a smooth batter.
4. Heat a poffertje pan and lightly grease indentations. Drop batter into the holes, cook for a few minutes and then flip over. If you don't have a poffertje pan, heat a large frying pan over medium-high heat with a dollop of butter and drop tablespoons of batter onto it and cook like mini pikelets. Add more butter as needed.
5. The poffertjes are cooked when golden on both sides.
6. Serve hot straight from the pan with globs of butter, a few blueberries, a sprig of thyme leaves and dusted with icing sugar.

CHEAT'S CHOCOLATE ECLAIRS

INGREDIENTS

1 cup (250ml, 8fl oz) thickened cream

125g (4oz) mascarpone

½ tsp vanilla extract

1 tsp icing sugar

1 tbsp cocoa powder

24 sponge finger biscuits

1 cup (250ml, 8fl oz) chocolate sauce (see recipe page 16)

1½ cups (150g, 5oz) blueberries

Mint leaves, to garnish

METHOD

1. Whip the cream until soft peaks form. Add the mascarpone, vanilla, sugar and cocoa and beat for 2 minutes on low or until thoroughly combined and smooth.

2. Pipe or place small dollops of chocolate cream along half the biscuits.

3. Gently press the remaining biscuits on top the chocolate cream.

4. Drizzle over the chocolate sauce and decorate with blueberries and mint leaves.

SERVES 2 ★ PREP 10MIN ★ COOK TIME 3MIN

CAKE IN A MUG

INGREDIENTS

4 tbsps plain flour

4 tbsps Dutch cocoa powder

1 tbsp caster sugar

1 egg, room temperature, lightly beaten

3 tbsps full cream milk

1 tbsp canola oil

¼ tsp vanilla extract

¼ cup (40g, 1½ oz) milk chocolate, chopped

2 tbsps caramel cream (see recipe page 19)

METHOD

1. Add the flour, cocoa and sugar to a small mixing bowl and stir well.

2. Pour in the egg, milk, oil and vanilla and whisk until well combined.

3. Divide the mix between 2 large mugs and microwave them together for 2½ minutes on high.

4. Sprinkle the milk chocolate over both mugs and drizzle over the caramel.

5. Wait a couple of minutes until the chocolate has melted, then serve.

KNICKERBOCKER GLORY

INGREDIENTS

1¼ cups (300ml, 10fl oz) thickened cream

1 tbsp caster sugar

1 tsp vanilla extract

1 cup (200g, 7oz) fresh strawberries, hulled and quartered

3 cups (750ml, 24fl oz) vanilla ice cream, softened

8 vanilla wafer straws

Strawberry sauce

¾ cup (150g, 5oz) fresh or frozen strawberries

¼ cup (55g, 2oz) caster sugar

½ tsp lemon juice

½ tbsp water

METHOD

1. To make the strawberry sauce add the strawberries, sugar, lemon juice and water to a small saucepan over low heat and cook for 8 minutes until the fruit starts to break apart. Remove from heat and set aside for 30 minutes to cool.

2. Puree the strawberries with a blender until you have a smooth puree. Press the puree through a sieve to remove the seeds and any solids. Spoon the sauce into a squirt bottle.

3. Whip the cream with the caster sugar and vanilla until stiff peaks form.

4. To assemble, squirt the sauce around the the inside of four serving glasses. Add a couple of strawberry quarters in the bottom and top them with a small scoop of icecream. Add a couple more strawberries over that and add another scoop of icecream and repeat.

5. Pile the whipped cream on the top of the glasses and decorate with strawberries and drizzle with sauce.

6. Stick two wafer straws into each glory and serve.

MARSHMALLOW SKEWERS WITH CHOCOLATE FONDUE

INGREDIENTS

400g (14oz) milk cooking chocolate, roughly chopped

1 cup (250ml, 8fl oz) thickened cream

280g (10oz) marshmallows, pink or white

Wooden skewers

METHOD

1. Soak the skewers in boiling water for 30 minutes before using – this prevents the wood from splintering.

2. Melt the chocolate and cream together in a heatproof bowl over a pot of simmering water for 10 minutes. Remove from heat

3. Place the marshmallows on the ends of the skewers, dip them in the melted chocolate and enjoy!

SERVES 8 ★ PREP 15MIN (PLUS CHILLING)

PISTACHIO AND ALMOND CHOCOLATE BARK

INGREDIENTS

300g (10oz) dark cooking chocolate, roughly chopped

2 small oranges, zested into thin 3cm (1in) strips, reserve a few strips

⅓ cup (40g, 1½ oz) pistachios, roughly chopped, reserve 1 tbsp

⅓ cup (40g, 1½ oz) toasted almonds, roughly chopped, reserve 1 tbsp

Pinch of sea salt flakes

METHOD

1. Place the chocolate in a large heatproof bowl over a pot of simmering water for 10 minutes or until melted. Remove from heat. Stir in the orange zest, pistachios, almonds and salt.

2. Line a large flat baking tray with baking paper.

3. Spread the melted chocolate mixture in a thin even layer on the paper with a flat spatula.

4. Press the reserved zest and nuts into the top.

5. Refrigerate for 2 hours, then break up into bite-size chunks with a knife and serve.

CHEAT'S CHEESECAKE

INGREDIENTS

Case

1-2 sheets store-bought frozen shortcrust pastry

1 tbsp milk, if needed

Filling

400g (14oz) mascarpone cheese

600g (1lb 5oz) vanilla fromage frais (Frûche)

Topping

1 cup (100g, 3½ oz) fresh or frozen blueberries

½ cup (60g, 2oz) fresh or frozen raspberries

2 tbsps icing sugar

Mint leaves, to garnish

METHOD

1. Remove the pastry from the freezer about 30 minutes before you want to use it, and allow to defrost.

2. Preheat the oven to 200°C (400°F, gas mark 6) and grease a 25cm loose-bottom fluted tart tin.

3. Press a whole sheet of pastry into the prepared tin. If required, cut strips from a second piece, and fill in any gaps allowing for some overlap. Lightly brush the area with milk. Place the strips in place and press together.

4. Blind bake for 15 minutes until pastry is dry. Remove the foil and beads and return to oven for a further 15 minutes. Remove from oven and set aside to cool completely.

5. Reduce oven to 160°C (325°F, Gas Mark 3).

6. To make the filling, beat together the mascarpone and Frûche until combined and smooth. Spread into the base and chill in the refrigerator for at least 2 hours.

7. Before serving, top with blueberries and raspberries. Garnish with some mint leaves and sift the icing sugar over the top.

COFFEE SYRUP PUDDING

INGREDIENTS

1½ cups (375ml, 13fl oz) milk

2 tbsps brewed espresso coffee, cooled

⅓ cup (55g, 2oz) chia seeds, reserve 1 tbsp

4 tbsps maple syrup

½ cup (60g, 2oz) pecans, half roughly chopped

¼ cup (50g, 2oz) cooked mashed pumpkin

¼ tsp cinnamon

¼ tsp allspice

¼ tsp vanilla extract

¼ cup (15g, ½ oz) cream

Mint leaves, to garnish

METHOD

1. Add the milk, coffee, chia seeds, 2 tablespoons of maple syrup and the chopped pecans to a large sealable jar and seal the lid tightly.

2. Shake vigorously until all ingredients are well combined.

3. Place the reserved chia seeds, remaining maple syrup, mashed pumpkin and spices in a small bowl and whisk vigorously to combine.

4. Divide the pumpkin mix between two serving glasses and then divide the coffee mixture in half and gently pour over the top of the pumpkin.

5. Refrigerate for at least 4 hours, preferably overnight.

6. Spoon a small amount of cream on top, garnish with mint and the remaining pecans and serve.

SERVES 2 ★ PREP 20MIN

CHERRY BANANA SPLIT

INGREDIENTS

¼ cup (60ml, 2fl oz) cherry syrup (see recipe page 62)

2 large ripe bananas

2 cups (500ml, 1pt) vanilla ice cream, softened

1½ cups (15g, ½ oz) salted caramel popcorn

1 cup (200g, 7oz) fresh cherries

METHOD

1. Cut the bananas in half lengthwise and divide between two serving bowls.

2. Top each with scoops of ice cream and scatter over the popcorn and cherries.

3. Drizzle over the cherry syrup and enjoy!

VANILLA CUPCAKES

INGREDIENTS

Cupcake batter

240g (8oz) unsalted
butter, room temperature

1 cup (240g, 8oz) caster
sugar

1½ tsps vanilla extract

2 medium eggs, room
temperature

2 tsps baking powder

2 cups (250g, 8oz) plain
flour

Buttercream icing

200g (7oz) unsalted
butter, room temperature

2½ cups (400g, 14oz)
pure icing sugar

4 tsps full cream milk

To decorate

2 cups (250g, 8oz)
fresh berries, such as
blueberries, raspberries,
redcurrants

mint leaves, to garnish

METHOD

1. Preheat the oven to 180°C (350°F, Gas Mark 4) and line two 12-hole cupcake tins with paper cases.

2. Beat the butter and sugar together until it resembles whipped cream. Add the vanilla and the eggs one at a time, completely mixing each one in before adding the next.

3. Sift the baking powder into the flour then sift the flour into the mixture in thirds, ensuring each portion is just mixed through before adding the next. It should be a thick batter. Add some milk if it's too thick. Divide the batter evenly between the 24 cases. (They should be half full.)

4. Bake in the oven for 12 minutes, or until a skewer inserted into the middle of one of the cakes comes out clean. Let cool for 10 minutes. Then place the individual cakes onto a wire rack to cool completely.

5. To make the icing, beat the butter for 3 minutes, then sift in the icing sugar in two portions, ensuring each portion is just mixed through before adding the next. Add half the milk and beat through. Add more only as needed until it's thick and smooth.

6. Top the cupcakes with the icing, then press your fruit into the top and garnish with mint leaves.

VANILLA CUSTARD

INGREDIENTS

1 vanilla bean, halved lengthways

1½ cups (375ml, 13fl oz) full cream milk

1 cup (250ml, 8fl oz) thickened cream

6 egg yolks, room temperature

½ cup (110g, 4oz) caster sugar

2 tsps arrowroot flour

METHOD

1. Scrape out the seeds from the vanilla bean with a teaspoon and place the seeds and bean halves a medium saucepan with the milk over low heat.

2. Stir for 3 minutes, then add the cream. Increase heat to medium and use a whisk to stir until almost simmering.

3. Remove from the heat, cover with a tight-fitting lid and sit for 15 minutes. Strain into a pouring jug.

4. Whisk together the egg yolks, sugar and flour in a medium saucepan for 5 minutes until pale and creamy and at least doubled in size. Pour in ¼ cup of the warm milk mixture and whisk through.

5. Heat the saucepan over medium heat and gradually whisk in the rest of milk mixture. Stir for 12 minutes or until the custard is thick enough to coat the back of a spoon.

6. Remove from heat and serve hot or cold

APPLE SAMOSA

INGREDIENTS

2 sheets puff pastry

3 medium Fuji or pink lady apples, peeled and cored

2 tbsps caster sugar

½ tsp ground cardamom

40g (1½ oz) unsalted butter, room temperature, cut into 1cm (½ in) cubes

2 egg whites, lightly beaten

2 tbsps sesame seeds

METHOD

1. Preheat the oven to 190°C (375°F, Gas Mark 5) and line a baking tray with baking paper.

2. Cut each sheet of pastry into four squares.

3. Halve the apples and cut into 5mm (¼ in) thick slices, then chop them into 2cm (1in) lengths. Toss the apples in a bowl with the sugar and cardamom.

4. Divide the apples between the 8 pastry squares, placing them on one diagonal half of each square (you want to fold them into triangles) and leaving a 5mm (¼ in) border free around them. Top the apples with cubes of butter.

5. Brush the edges of the pastry with water and fold over the squares to form a triangle. Use a fork to press down on the edges to seal them.

6. Brush the tops with egg whites and sprinkle the sesame seeds over the top. Bake for 17 minutes or until golden brown.

7. Serve warm.

CHOCOLATE PEPPERMINT SLICE

INGREDIENTS

250g (9oz) chocolate ripple biscuits

80g (3oz) unsalted butter, melted

2¼ cups (360g, 13oz) icing sugar, sifted

2 tbsps full cream milk

160g (6oz) Copha, roughly chopped

1½ tsps peppermint essence

375g (13oz) cooking chocolate (milk, not dark), roughly chopped

50g (2oz) unsalted butter, roughly chopped

METHOD

1. Line a 20 x 30cm (8 x 12in) slice tin with greased baking paper.

2. To make the base, add the biscuits to a food processor and process until it resembles breadcrumbs. Pour in the melted butter and pulse a couple of times to combine. Press the mix in a smooth even layer in the bottom of the tin. Chill for at least 40 minutes before moving onto the next step.

3. Add the sugar, milk and half the Copha to a saucepan and heat over medium-low heat for at least 8 minutes or until melted and smooth. Stir through the peppermint essence. Remove from heat and immediately pour over the base. Chill for at least 1 hour or until firm before moving on to the next step.

4. Place the chocolate and butter in a large heatproof bowl over a pot of simmering water for 10 minutes or until melted.

5. Pour over the peppermint layer and then chill the slice in the refrigerator for at least 4 hours, preferably overnight.

6. Cut into roughly 4cm (1½ in) squares and serve.

MAKES 4 ★ PREP 20min (PLUS CHILLING) ★ COOK TIME 5min

BANANA LOGS

INGREDIENTS

¾ cup (50g, 2oz) almonds, chopped

1 tsp honey

¼ tsp ground cardamom (optional)

¾ cup (170g, 6oz) Greek yoghurt

2 ripe but firm bananas, peeled and halved

4 wooden icy-pole sticks

METHOD

1. Heat a small frying pan or saucepan to medium-high. Dry-cook the almonds for 3 minutes, stirring constantly or until they are just browned. Remove from the pan immediately and set aside to cool.

2. In a small bowl, thoroughly mix the honey and cardamom, if using, into the yoghurt.

3. Gently insert the sticks into the cut ends of the bananas. Line a large flat baking tray with baking paper.

4. Place the yoghurt onto a small plate and do the same with the almonds. Roll the bananas in spiced yoghurt to coat them. Then gently roll each yoghurt banana in the almonds to lightly coat. Sprinkle some on top while you roll. Place the bananas on the tray and place in the freezer for a minimum of 1 hour, but ideally overnight.

BANANA NICECREAM

INGREDIENTS

4 large very ripe bananas

½ tsp vanilla essence

¼ tsp allspice

METHOD

1. Line a large flat baking tray with baking paper.

2. Peel the bananas and chop into 1cm (½ in) slices.

3. Arrange the slices on the tray and freeze for at least 3 hours.

4. Add the slices into a high-speed food processor or blender. Puree the banana until you have a smooth frozen puree. Add the vanilla and allspice and mix through.

5. Serve immediately or return to the freezer to chill for 2 hours for a thicker ice-cream consistency.

   Note: If you're having trouble getting the bananas to puree, try letting the slices thaw for 20 minutes, puree, then freeze for 30 minutes and puree again.

SERVES 6 ★ PREP 15MIN (PLUS CHILLING) ★ COOK TIME 20MIN

MERINGUE CREAM ROULADE

INGREDIENTS

4 egg whites, room temperature

1 cup (200g, 7oz) caster sugar

1 tsp white vinegar

2 tsps cream of tartar

2 tbsps icing sugar

2 cups (500ml, 1pt) thickened cream

1 cup (125g, 4oz) fresh or frozen raspberries

1 cup (100g, 3½ oz) fresh or frozen blueberries

½ cup (50g, 2oz) fresh or frozen redcurrants

METHOD

1. Preheat the oven to 160°C (325°F, Gas Mark 3) and line a 25 x 30cm (10 x 12in) Swiss roll tin with greased baking paper.

2. Beat the egg whites until soft peaks form. Add the sugar into the mixture in thirds, ensuring each portion is just mixed through before adding the next, until the sugar is thoroughly combined and stiff peaks form. Beat in the vinegar and cream of tartar.

3. Spoon the meringue into the tin and spread out into an even layer. Bake for 15 minutes until a crust forms. Remove from the oven and let the meringue cool for 10 minutes.

4. Spread out a tea towel onto a work surface. Cut out a large rectangle of baking paper (larger than the roll tin) and dust with half the icing sugar. Gently flip the meringue onto the baking paper. Let it cool for 30 minutes.

5. Beat the cream with the rest of the icing sugar until soft peaks form. Spread half the cream over the meringue. Dot the cream with ¼ cup each of the raspberries and blueberries.

6. Carefully roll up the meringue, peeling back the tea towel and baking paper as you go. Chill in the refrigerator for 1 hour.

7. To serve, top with the rest of the whipped cream and decorate with the rest of the berries, some mint leaves and edible flowers.

COCONUT MACAROONS

INGREDIENTS

1 cup (90g, 3oz) desiccated coconut

1 cup (90g, 3oz) shredded coconut

2 egg whites, room temperature

⅓ cup (70g, 2½ oz) caster sugar

1 tsp almond extract

Pinch of salt

METHOD

1. Preheat the oven to 180°C (350°F, Gas Mark 4) and line a large flat baking tray with baking paper.

2. Spread the coconut over the baking tray and toast in the oven for 5 minutes. Remove immediately and tip into a container and replace the paper back on the tray.

3. Whisk together the egg whites, sugar, almond extract and salt until the sugar has dissolved. Stir through the toasted coconut.

4. Shape dessertspoons of the mixture into small rounded pyramids and place on the tray. Leave about 5mm (¼ in) space between each.

5. Bake for 12 minutes or until they're golden brown.

6. Let cool for 30 minutes before serving.

EASY PEACH TRIFLE

INGREDIENTS

1½ cups (375ml, 13fl oz) thickened cream

1 tbsp caster sugar

½ tsp vanilla extract

1 small store-bought vanilla sponge cake, broken into bite-size pieces

4 medium yellow peaches, halved and stoned, and cut into 8 slices

1½ cups (150g, 5oz) fresh blueberries

1 cup (250ml, 8fl oz) thickened custard

METHOD

1. Whip the cream with the sugar and vanilla until soft peaks form.

2. Divide half the sponge cake between four dessert glasses.

3. Place three peach slices and a couple of blueberries on top of the cake.

4. Top with 1½ tablespoons of custard, then with 1 tablespoon of whipped cream and then a couple more blueberries

5. Top with another tablespoon of cream, then the rest of the cake. Top that with four slices of peach, another 1½ tablespoons of custard and then with the rest of the whipped cream.

6. Refrigerate for at least 2 hours to let cake soak up the custard and cream.

7. Garnish each glass with some blueberries, a slice of peach and a sprinkle of sugar if desired before serving.

GUILT-FREE

RAW CARROT AND PISTACHIO CAKE

INGREDIENTS

Icing

2 cups (250g, 8oz) raw cashews

4 cups (1L, 2pt) water

3 tbsps coconut oil

4 tbsps agave syrup

2 tsps vanilla extract

2 tbsps lemon juice

Pinch of salt

Cake

2 cups (100g, 3½ oz) carrots, grated

½ cup (60g, 2oz) walnuts, finely chopped

(90g, 3oz) pistachios, finely chopped, reserve ¼ cup for topping

2 cups (350g, 12oz) Medjool dates, pitted and roughly chopped

½ cup (40g, 1½ oz) desiccated coconut

1 tsp vanilla extract

¼ tsp cinnamon

¼ tsp allspice

¼ tsp ground cloves

¼ tsp ground cardamom

METHOD

1. Start on the icing the night before. Soak the cashews in the water overnight.

2. Place all the icing ingredients in a blender and blend to a smooth thick paste. Set aside.

3. Add all the cake ingredients to a food processor and process to a thick paste. Divide in half and press half into the bottom of a 23cm (9in) springform cake tin in a smooth, even layer.

4. Spread one third of the icing over the cake mix in an even layer. Then spread the rest of the cake mixture on top of the icing in an even layer.

5. Spread the rest of the icing over the top.

6. Chill in the fridge for at least 2 hours to let the cake set.

7. Sprinkle with the reserved chopped pistachios and serve.

VEGAN CHOC POTS

INGREDIENTS

1 tbsp coconut oil

2 x 400g (14oz) cans coconut milk

¾ cup (235g, 8oz) agave syrup

½ cup (85g, 3oz) chia seeds

1 tbsp cacao powder

For garnishing

Raspberries

Slivered almonds

Mint leaves

METHOD

1. Whisk together all the pudding ingredients for 3 minutes until thoroughly combined.

2. Pour into six serving glasses and refrigerate for at least 4 hours, preferably overnight.

3. Serve topped with blueberries, almonds and mint leaves.

SERVES 2 ★ PREP 10min (PLUS CHILLING)

BERRY COCOWHIP

INGREDIENTS

1 cup (250ml, 8fl oz) coconut yoghurt

1 cup (100g, 3½ oz) frozen blueberries

1 small frozen banana, roughly chopped

½ tsp vanilla extract

1½ tbsps agave syrup

2 tbsps coconut water

METHOD

1. Place the yoghurt, blueberries, banana, vanilla and agave into a blender and blend until you have smooth thick puree.

2. Add the coconut water only as needed if you need to make the consistency thinner.

3. Transfer to an airtight container and freeze for 15 minutes.

4. Serve chilled topped with extra blueberries or other summer fruits.

MATCHA MACARONS

INGREDIENTS

Filling

1½ tsps matcha green tea powder

⅓ cup (80ml, 3fl oz) thickened cream

20g (¾ oz) unsalted butter, room temperature and chopped into small cubes

100g (3½ oz) white cooking chocolate, roughly chopped

Shells

100g (3½ oz) fresh egg whites, room temperature

¼ cup (60g, 2oz) caster sugar

1 cup (110g, 4oz) almond meal

2 tsps matcha powder

1 cup (160g, 5oz) pure icing sugar

Green food colouring

METHOD

1. Line two large flat baking trays with baking paper.

2. To make the filling, whisk together the matcha powder and the cream in a small saucepaon over medium-low heat. Whisk for about 5 minutes until the powder is dissolved and the mixture is almost simmering. Remove from heat.

3. Add the butter and chocolate and let sit for 5 minutes, then gently stir until the chocolate and butter are incorporated. Set aside.

4. To make the shells, beat the egg whites until stiff peaks form. Then slowly pour in the caster sugar, beating as you pour. The sugar should be completely dissolved and the meringue should be glossy and stiff.

5. Use a whisk to stir in the almond meal, matcha powder, icing sugar and a couple of drops of food colouring through the meringue. Be vigorous and ensure the mixture is combined and thick and creamy. Then let it sit for 15 minutes.

6. Spoon the mix into a piping bag with a 1cm (½ in) tip. Pipe the mixture onto the trays in 3cm (1in) rounds and leave at least 3cm (1in) space between each.

7. Let the tray sit for around 1 hour until the tops don't stick to your finger when you touch them.

8. Preheat the oven to 180°C (350°F, Gas Mark 4). Put the macarons into the oven and reduce the temperature to 160°C (325°F, Gas Mark 3). Bake for 15 minutes. They should be cooked, but don't let them brown. Remove and let them cool to room temperature.

10. Spread slightly less than a teaspoon of the matcha filling on the flat side of half the macarons. Gently press the other halves on top to form the macarons.

MANGO CHIA PUDDING

INGREDIENTS

Mango puree

4 large mangoes, peeled and cut off the seed, reserve 1 cup (165g, 6oz) cubed mango

4 tbsps desiccated coconut

⅓ cup (105g, 4oz) agave syrup

2½ cups (600ml, 21fl oz) coconut milk

¾ cup (125g, 4oz) chia seeds

2 tsps vanilla extract

½ tsp ground cardamom

6 sprigs of mint, to garnish

METHOD

1. Puree the mango flesh together with the desiccated coconut and 3 tablespoons of the agave syrup in a blender until you get a smooth puree.

2. Whisk together rest of the agave, the coconut milk, chia seeds, vanilla and cardamom in a large mixing bowl.

3. Whisk through the mango puree until thoroughly combined. Adjust sweetness with more agave syrup if needed.

4. Divide the pudding mix between six dessert glasses and place in the refrigerator for at least 4 hours, preferably overnight.

5. Serve topped with the chopped mango, a sprinkle of extra chia seeds and a sprig of mint.

SERVES 4 ★ PREP 30MIN (PLUS CHILLING)

BLACK FOREST POTS

INGREDIENTS

1 cup (60g, 2oz) whipped coconut cream

¼ cup (40g, 1½ oz) shaved dark chocolate

Chocolate sauce

2 medium ripe avocados

¼ cup (30g, 1oz) cacao powder

¼ cup (80g, 3oz) agave syrup

½ tsp vanilla extract

Pinch of salt

Cherries in sauce

1 cup (200g, 7oz) cherries, stoned and chopped, plus 8 whole cherries, with stems intact

2 tsps agave syrup

Pudding

6 tbsps black chia seeds

2 cups (500ml, 1pt) coconut water

1 tsp vanilla extract

3 tbsps agave syrup

METHOD

1. To make the chocolate sauce, place all of the ingredients in a food processor or blender and blend until completely smooth.

2. Roughly mash the chopped cherries together with the agave syrup. They should still be chunky, but there should be some liquid.

3. Whisk together all the pudding ingredients in a mixing bowl. Divide between four dessert glasses and refrigerate for at least 4 hours, preferably overnight.

4. To assemble, spoon even portions of whipped cream over the chia pudding. Top with even portions of cherries in syrup. Spoon over the chocolate sauce. Top with the whole cherries and sprinkle over the shaved chocolate.

GREEN TEA PANNA COTTA WITH RED BEANS

INGREDIENTS

Panna cotta

2 tsps gelatine powder

1 cup (250ml, 8fl oz) low-fat milk

1 tbsp agave syrup

1 tsp matcha green tea powder

1 cup (250ml, 8fl oz) low-fat vanilla yoghurt

Red bean mash

½ cup (115g, 4oz) dried red beans

6 cups (1.5L, 50fl oz) water

¼ cup (80g, 3oz) agave syrup

Mint leaves, to garnish

METHOD

1. To make the panna cotta place 2 tablespoons of chilled water into a small bowl and slowly sprinkle the gelatine in. Let it sit for 10 minutes.

2. Place the milk, syrup and matcha powder into a small saucepan over medium heat. Gently whisk until almost simmering. Remove from heat and whisk in the gelatine until dissolved. Let cool for 15 minutes.

3. Whisk in the yoghurt thoroughly. Lightly oil four serving glasses and distribute the mixture evenly between the four glasses.

4. Cover with plastic wrap and chill in the refrigerator for at least 3 hours to firm up.

5. To make the red bean mash, put the beans and 3 cups of water in a small saucepan. Bring to a boil, then drain the beans.

6. Wash the saucepan and place the beans in it again with another 3 cups of water. Bring to a boil, then immediately reduce the heat to low and simmer, covered, for 1½ hours, adding more water as needed to keep the beans submerged. Once the beans are soft, drain them and return to the pot.

7. Heat over medium heat, add the agave and stir through for 5 minutes. Remove from the heat and roughly mash. Add more agave to taste. Let cool for at least 1 hour.

8. Serve the panna cotta with a spoonful of red beans and some mint leaves to garnish.

PUMPKIN CUSTARD POTS

INGREDIENTS

4 cups (550g, 1¼ lb) butternut pumpkin, peeled and cut into 3cm (1in) chunks

7g (¼ oz) gelatine powder

¼ cup (60ml, 2fl oz) boiling water

1 x 400g (14oz) can of coconut milk

⅓ cup (105g, 4oz) agave syrup

1 tsp vanilla extract

½ tsp cinnamon

½ tsp allspice

¼ tsp nutmeg

¼ tsp ground cloves

METHOD

1. Preheat the oven to 160°C (325°F, Gas Mark 3) and line a large flat baking tray with baking paper. Scatter the pumpkin over the tray in an even layer and bake for 40 minutes or until softened. Place the baked pumpkin in a blender and puree.

2. Stir the gelatine into the hot water and set aside.

3. Add the coconut milk, pumpkin, agave, vanilla and spices to a medium pot and heat over medium heat until almost simmering. Adjust to taste with more agave if needed.

4. Remove from the heat and whisk in the gelatine.

5. Divide the custard between six ramekins and let cool for 30 minutes.

6. Place the ramekins in the refrigerator and chill for at least 3 hours so the custard can set before serving.

SOY MILK PUDDING

INGREDIENTS

Pudding

2 tsps gelatine powder

3 tbsps boiling water

2½ cups (600ml, 21fl oz) soy milk

3 tbsps caster sugar

¼ cup (80g, 3oz) pure maple syrup

METHOD

1. Stir together the gelatine and water in a small bowl. Set aside.

2. Whisk the soy milk and sugar in a medium saucepan over medium heat until almost simmering.

3. Remove from the heat and whisk in the gelatine liquid until dissolved.

4. Pour the mixture into a large bowl, cover with plastic wrap and chill in the refrigerator for at least 4 hours, preferably overnight.

5. Serve chilled with a spoonful of maple syrup over the top.

VEGAN CHOCOLATE CAKE

INGREDIENTS

Cake

4 cups (500g, 1lb) plain flour

1 cup (110g, 4oz) cacao powder

2½ tsps bicarbonate of soda

1 tsp salt

1 tsp allspice

2½ tbsps apple cider vinegar

2¾ cups (685ml, 24fl oz) soy milk

1 cup (250ml, 8fl oz) coconut oil, melted

2 tsps vanilla extract

2 cups (300g, 10oz) coconut sugar

1 tbsp pure maple syrup

Chocolate icing

1⅓ cups (330ml, 11fl oz) coconut milk

¼ cup (80g, 3oz) pure maple syrup

450g (1lb) unsweetened dark cooking chocolate, roughly chopped

METHOD

1. Preheat the oven to 180°C (350°F, Gas Mark 4) and grease three 20cm (8in) springform cake tins with coconut oil and dust with cacao powder.

2. Place the flour, cacao, bicarb, salt and allspice into a large mixing bowl and give it a couple of stirs.

3. In a separate mixing bowl, beat together the apple cider and the milk until it's light and frothy. Whisk in the oil, vanilla, sugar and maple syrup.

4. Add the dry ingredients into the wet mixture in thirds, ensuring each portion is just mixed through before adding the next. Don't mix too much.

5. Divide the cake batter between the three cake tins and bake for 20 minutes or until a skewer inserted into the middle comes out clean.

6. Remove the cakes from the tins and let them cool to room temperature on a wire rack.

7. To make the icing, gently whisk the coconut milk and maple syrup together in a small saucepan over medium-high heat until barely simmering. Place the chocolate in a large mixing bowl and pour the heated milk over it. Let it sit for 3 minutes, then gently stir until the chocolate is melted and ingredients are all combined. Allow to cool to room temperature, giving it a gentle stir every now and then. You want it to still drip when you use it to ice the cake.

8. Ice the bottom cake layer with just over a quarter of the icing mixture. Place the second cake on top and again ice with just over a quarter of the icing. Place the third layer on top and use the rest of the icing over that.

BLUEBERRY COCONUT CRUMBLE

INGREDIENTS

1 cup (75g, 3oz) rolled oats

¼ cup (20g, ¾ oz) coconut flakes

¼ cup (30g, 1oz) almond meal

1 tsp cinnamon

1½ tbsps pure maple syrup

25g (1oz) unsalted butter, room temperature

6 cups (600g, 1lb 5oz) frozen blueberries

3 tbsps arrowroot flour

2 tsps vanilla extract

METHOD

1. Preheat the oven to 180°C (350°F, Gas Mark 4) and lightly grease a 23cm (9in) round deep pie dish.

2. Place the oats and coconut flakes in a food processor and blend until they resemble breadcrumbs, don't make them any finer than that. Add the almond meal, cinnamon, maple syrup and butter and pulse a couple of times until the maple syrup and butter is mixed through.

3. Toss the blueberries in a large bowl with the arrowroot flour and vanilla.

4. Transfer the blueberries to the to pie dish and top with the oat mixture. Bake for 35 minutes or until the topping is lightly browned.

5. Serve warm or cold.

CHOCOLATE AVOCADO MOUSSE

INGREDIENTS

3 large avocados

⅓ cup (80ml, 3fl oz) soy milk

⅓ cup (105g, 4oz) pure maple syrup

1 tbsp agave syrup

¼ cup (30g, 1oz) cacao powder

¼ cup (60ml, 2fl oz) coconut oil

½ tsp allspice

Mint leaves, to garnish

METHOD

1. Scoop out the avocado flesh and add to a food processor with the rest of the ingredients.

2. Blend until you have a smooth, silky mixture.

3. Divide evenly between serving glasses, cover with plastic wrap and chill in the refrigerator for at least 3 hours before serving.

4. Serve garnished with mint leaves.

PEANUT BUTTER CUPS

INGREDIENTS

½ cup (125ml, 4fl oz) coconut oil, melted

½ cup (60g, 2oz) raw cacao powder

4 tbsps agave syrup

⅓ cup (85g, 3oz) sugar-free peanut butter

METHOD

1. Line a mini muffin tin with mini cupcake liners.

2. Whisk together the coconut oil, cacao and agave syrup. (add more agave if not sweet enough).

3. Pour small amounts of the chocolate mix into the bottom of each cupcake liner. (Use just under half the chocolate mixture for this.)

4. Place the pan in the refrigerator for 30 minutes to harden.

5. Place a small amount of peanut butter (about half a teaspoon) in the centre of each round of chilled chocolate. Flatten it slightly but leave about 2mm (⅛ in) free around the edge.

6. Heat the chocolate mixture if needed to make it runny. Pour enough chocolate over each portion of peanut butter to just cover it.

7. Return the tray to the freezer and chill for at least 2 hours until the chocolate has hardened.

RAW CHOCOLATE TART

INGREDIENTS

Base

1½ cups (135g, 5oz) hazelnut flour

¼ cup (30g, 1oz) cacao powder

3 Medjool dates, pitted

2 tsps maple syrup

2 tbsps coconut oil

Pinch of salt

Filling

3 medium avocados

⅓ cup (80ml, 3fl oz) soy milk

⅓ cup (105g, 4oz) pure maple syrup

1 tbsp golden syrup

½ cup (60g, 2oz) cacao powder

¼ cup (60ml, 2fl oz) coconut oil

½ tsp allspice

1 cup (200g, 7oz) fresh strawberries, halved

METHOD

1. To make the base, add the hazelnut flour and cacao powder to the bowl of a food processor and pulse a couple of times to mix through. Add the rest of the base ingredients and process until the mixture starts to come together.

2. Press into the bottom and sides of a fluted 23cm (9in) pie tin with a removable base. Place in the refrigerator to chill for 20 minutes.

3. To make the filling, puree all the filling ingredients together until you have a smooth, silky mixture.

4. Spoon the filling onto the base and smooth the top. Refrigerate for at least 3 hours until it sets.

5. To serve, remove the cake from the tin and garnish with fresh strawberries.

VEGAN KEY LIME PIE

INGREDIENTS

Pie crust

1 cup (125g, 4oz) raw macadamias

½ cup (40g, 1½ oz) shredded coconut

½ cup (85g, 3oz) Medjool dates, pitted and roughly chopped

¼ cup (40g, 1½ oz) ground flaxseed

2 tbsps coconut oil, melted

½ tsp salt

¼ tsp ground ginger

Filling

1½ cups (185g, 6oz) raw cashews

7 medium limes

½ cup (125ml, 4fl oz) coconut oil, melted

1 cup (250ml, 8fl oz) coconut cream

Pinch of salt

²/₃ cup (210g, 8oz) pure maple syrup

¼ tsp green food colouring

METHOD

1. Lightly oil the base and line the sides of a 22cm springform cake tin.

2. Place the macadamias and coconut in a food processor and process into a thick paste. Add the dates and pulse a few times to mix through. Add the rest of the pie crust ingredients and pulse a few more times to mix together.

3. Press the mixture into the bottom of the cake tin and refrigerate until you're ready to pour the filling onto it.

4. To make the filling, soak the cashews in water for at least 4 hours, preferably overnight.

5. Finely zest six of the limes and juice four of them. Cut the last lime into thin slices.

6. Place the juice, half the zest, the drained cashews, coconut oil, coconut cream, salt and maple syrup in a food processer and process until you have a thick smooth filling.

7. Reserve ¾ cup of the filling and transfer the rest to the cake tin and smooth over.

8. Mix the food colouring in with the reserved filling and spread over the top of the filling.

9. Chill in the refrigerator for 1 hour before serving. Decorate with the remaining zest and lime slices.

FRUIT PIZZA

INGREDIENTS

Base

1½ cups (130g, 4½ oz) rolled oats

3 medium ripe bananas, mashed

⅓ cup (40g, 1½ oz) almond meal

3 tbsps agave syrup

Pizza sauce

½ cup (125ml, 4fl oz) coconut cream

¼ cup (60ml, 2fl oz) Greek yoghurt

Toppings

1 cup (200g, 7oz) strawberries, hulled and halved

½ cup (60g, 2oz) fresh raspberries

½ cup (50g, 2oz) blueberries

1 kiwi fruit, peeled and sliced

METHOD

1. Preheat oven to 190°C (375°F, Gas Mark 5) and line a large flat baking tray with baking paper.

2. Mix together the oats, bananas, almond meal and agave.

3. Spread out in a large circle to fit a pizza pan and bake for 25-30 minutes until browned and cooked through. Let cool to room temperature.

4. Whisk together the coconut cream and yoghurt until thoroughly combined. Spread over the pizza base.

5. Arrange fruit on top of the pizza and add any other fruit as desired.

PASSIONFRUIT MOUSSE

INGREDIENTS

8 passionfruit

1½ tbsps lime juice, strained

4 tsps gelatine powder

1¼ cups (300ml, 10fl oz) light cream

¼ cup (80g, 3oz) agave syrup

½ tsp vanilla extract

1¼ cups (300ml, 10fl oz) thick Greek yoghurt

METHOD

1. Place the pulp from seven of the passionfruit into a food processor and process for about 10 seconds. Push the blended mix through a strainer and discard the solids. You need ½ cup of juice. Set aside.

2. Stir the lime juice and gelatine powder together in a bowl. Set aside.

3. Mix together the cream, syrup and vanilla in a small saucepan over medium-high heat until nearly boiling. Remove from heat and whisk the lime juice and gelatine through for 1 minute. Let cool for 30 minutes.

4. Add the passionfruit juice and yoghurt and again whisk to mix through.

5. Pour into four dessert glasses, cover them with plastic wrap and then refrigerate for at least 4 hours, preferably overnight.

6. Serve topped with a teaspoon of pulp from the remaining passionfruit.

VEGAN CHOCOLATE COOKIES

INGREDIENTS

Cookies

4 tbsps ground flaxseed

¾ cup (235g, 8oz) pure maple syrup

2½ cups (310g, 10oz) walnuts halves

½ cup (60g, 2oz) cacao powder

¼ tsp salt

1 tbsp vanilla extract

Vegan chocolate spread

200g (7oz) firm tofu

¼ cup (30g, 1oz) cacao powder

⅓ cup (50g, 2oz) brown sugar

2 tbsps agave syrup

25 walnut halves for decoration

METHOD

1. Preheat the oven to 180°C (350°F, Gas Mark 4) and line a large flat baking tray with baking paper.

2. Place the flaxseed in a food processor and grind to a meal. Remove to a large mixing bowl. Add the maple syrup and mix through.

3. Process 2 cups of the walnuts in batches until they resemble fine breadcrumbs. Add to the mixing bowl along with the cacao powder, salt and vanilla. Lightly process the remaining walnuts to rough crumbs. Add to the mixing bowl.

4. Mix everything through thoroughly. Place round tablespoons of the cookie mix onto the baking tray and flatten out with about 2cm (1in) between each as they don't spread much.

    Bake for 15 minutes and let them cool on the tray before removing from the sheet.

5. To make the chocolate spread, place the tofu, cacao and brown sugar in a food processer and blend until completely smooth. Then drizzle in the agave while blending until smooth and silky.

6. Place a teaspoon of chocolate spread on each cookie and press a walnut half into it. Enjoy!

SEMOLINA BERRY PUDDING

INGREDIENTS

1 cup (125g, 4oz) fresh or frozen blackberries, reserve 4 for garnish

1 cup (250ml, 8fl oz) coconut milk

1 cup (250ml, 8fl oz) water

½ cup (175g, 6oz) semolina flour

1 tsp vanilla extract

¼ cup (80g, 3oz) agave syrup

METHOD

1. Place the blackberries in a blender and roughly blend. You still want solids, it shouldn't be a puree. Set aside.

2. Pour the coconut milk and water into a medium saucepan and bring to a boil over medium heat.

3. Slowly pour in the semolina while continuously whisking. Simmer for 5 minutes, stirring continuously (the porridge will 'spit' if you let it boil without stirring).

4. Remove from the heat and stir through the vanilla and blackberries.

5. Whisk the mixture for 5 minutes until it is light and fluffy. Sweeten to taste with the agave.

6. Pour into four small pudding moulds and chill in the refrigerator for at least 4 hours, preferably overnight.

7. Turn the puddings out onto serving plates and top with a blackberry each just before serving.

MALABI TURKISH DESSERT

INGREDIENTS

Pudding

5 tbsps arrowroot flour

1 tsp rosewater

2¼ cups (560ml, 19 fl oz) coconut milk

½ cup (125ml, 4fl oz) thickened cream

3 tbsps agave syrup

¼ cup (30g, 1oz) pistachios, roughly chopped

¼ cup (20g, ¾ oz) desiccated coconut

Rosewater syrup

½ cup (155g, 5oz) agave syrup

1 cup (250ml, 8fl oz) water

1 tsp lemon juice

2 tbsps rosewater

Red food colouring

METHOD

1. Stir arrowroot flour and rosewater into ½ cup of the coconut milk.

2. Pour the rest of the milk into a medium saucepan along with the cream and agave over medium-high heat. Reduce the heat to low, give the flour mix another quick stir and pour into the saucepan. Stir constantly until the mixture thickens to a cream.

3. Divide the mixture between four dessert glasses and let them cool for 30 minutes. Then cover with plastic wrap and place in the refrigerator to chill or at least 4 hours, preferably overnight.

4. To make the syrup, place the agave, water and lemon juice in small saucepan over medium-high heat and bring to a boil. Reduce to a simmer and cook for 10 minutes until it thickens to a syrup.

5. Remove from heat and stir in the rosewater and two drops of food colouring. Let cool to room temperature.

6. Serve the puddings with the syrup drizzled over and topped with pistachios and coconut.

PUMPKIN DOUGHNUTS

INGREDIENTS

Pumpkin puree

2 cups (270g, 9oz) butternut pumpkin, peeled and cut into 3cm (1in) chunks

¼ tsp cinnamon

¼ tsp allspice

Pinch of nutmeg

Pinch of ground cloves

Doughnuts

1½ cups (185g, 6oz) plain flour

½ tsp salt

1½ tsps baking powder

½ cup (155g, 5oz) agave syrup

2½ tbsps coconut oil, melted

½ cup (125ml, 4fl oz) soy milk

2 tbsps pure maple syrup, for glazing

METHOD

1. To make the pumpkin puree, preheat the oven to 160°C (325°F, Gas Mark 3) and line a large flat baking tray with baking paper. Scatter the pumpkin over the tray in an even layer and bake for 40 minutes or until softened. Place the baked pumpkin in a blender and puree together with the cinnamon, allspice, nutmeg and cloves. You need ⅓ cup of puree for this recipe.

2. Increase the oven temperature to 180°C (350°F, Gas Mark 4) and generously oil a doughnut pan with coconut oil. Set aside.

3. In a large mixing bowl whisk together the dry ingredients and make a well in the middle. In a separate bowl whisk together ⅓ cup puree, agave, coconut oil and soy milk. Pour the wet ingredients into the dry and mix together until just combined.

4. Spoon the batter into the doughnut pan and bake for 13 minutes or until the dough springs back when lightly pressed. Let the doughnuts cool for 5 minutes in the pan before placing them on a wire rack.

5. Brush with maple syrup to glaze and serve warm or cold.

INDEX

First Published in 2018 by Herron Book Distributors Pty Ltd
14 Manton St
Morningside
 QLD 4170
www.herronbooks.com

Custom book production by Captain Honey Pty Ltd
12 Station Street
Bangalow
NSW 2479
www.captainhoney.com.au

Cataloguing-in-Publication. A catalogue record for this book is available from the National Library of Australia

ISBN 978-0-947163-80-8

Printed and bound in China by 1010 Printing International Limited

5 4 3 2   19 20 21 22

NOTES FOR THE READER

Preparation, cooking times and serving sizes vary according to the skill, agility and appetite of the cook and should be used as a guide only.

All reasonable efforts have been made to ensure the accuracy of the content in this book. Information in this book is not intended as a substitute for medical advice. The author and publisher cannot and do not accept any legal duty of care or responsibility in relation to the content in this book, and disclaim any liabilities relating to its use.

PHOTO CREDITS

Front cover: Gabriela Popa
Back cover: marcin jucha
Images used under license from Shutterstock.com
18042011 p243. 5 second Studio p205. Africa Studio p9,14,51,73,99,143,196. AGCreations p104,211.Alfa Photostudio p185. Alp Aksoy p177. Amawasri Pakdara p237. AnaMarques p165. Angela Llorente p231. Anna-Mari West p242. Anna_Pustynnikova p135,169. Anna Shepulova p11,13,41,61,123,159. Anna Shkuratova p67. AS Food studio p43,55,181. Barbara Dudzinska p61,131. Barbara Neveu p139. Bartosz Luczak p21,25,105,208. bitt24 p203. bonchan p26. Brent Hofacker p53,71,173,233,239. CKP1001 p142. Dejan Stanic Micko p85. Edith Frincu p241. Elena Veselova p37,63,81,93,94,149,197,222. Elena Zajchikova p121. Ekaterina Glazova p111,127,136,145,153. Fascinadora p161. Flaffy p115. Fortyforks p2.Foxys Forest Manufacture p75,133. Gabriela Popa p59. Gaus Alex p17,19, 86,172. GeNik p209. hadasit p251. Ildi Papp p39. inewsfoto p16. In Green p58. Innershadows Photography p117. Irina Barcari p119. Irina Goleva p125. Irina Meliukh p33,65,79,217. Iryna Melnyk p7,187,189,225. iuliia_n p212. Ivanna Grigorova p77. Jack Jelly p163. JiJaJuNg p193. JRP Studio p213. July Prokopiv p254. kariphoto p250. Lesya Dolyuk p23,49,155,235. Liliya Kandrashevich p141. Iocrifa p253. Lyudmila Mikhailovskaya p229. MaraZe p15. marcin jucha p151. Mariela Naplatanova p6,Maslova Valentina p95. Maya Morenko p27. msheldrake p25. MShev p113. MSPhotographic p214. Nataliya Arzamasova p103,190,247. NatalyaBond p207. Natalya Maiorova p129. Natasha Breen p6,58,108,148,179,184,220. neil langan p170. ninikas p83. NoirChocolate p206. Oksana Mizina p31. Olga Miltsova p24. Oxana Denezhkina p87. Paul_Brighton p50. Paul Rich Studio p76. pinkdollarz p227. Richard M Lee p199. sarsmis p45, 69,137, 92. SEAGULL_L p101,215. Simxa p249. Siim79 p167. SMarina p89. Stepanek Photography p47. stockcreations p180,195. Tatiana Vorona p138. TorriPhoto p62. trebornov p88. Truengtra Paejai p171. VasiliyBudarin p97. Vitaly Goncharov p201. vm2002 p228. yari2000 p30. Yulia-Bogdanova p81. YuliiaHolovchenko p224. zarzamora p164,174,223. zkruger p29,35. zoryanchik p157.
Unsplash © Alexander Mils p109. Edgar Castrejon p221. Norwood Themes p91. Sheri Silver p175. Taylor Kiser p198.